Essential Histories

# The First World War

The Eastern Front 1914–1918

# Essential Histories

# The First World War

## The Eastern Front 1914–1918

Geoffrey Jukes

OSPREY
PUBLISHING

First published in Great Britain in 2002 by Osprey Publishing,
Elms Court, Chapel Way, Botley, Oxford OX2 9LP

Email: info@ospreypublishing.com

ISBN 1 84176 342 X

Editor: Rebecca Cullen
Design: Ken Vail Graphic Design, Cambridge, UK
Cartography by The Map Studio
Index by Alan Thatcher
Picture research by Image Select International
Origination by Grasmere Digital Imaging, Leeds, UK
Printed and bound in China by L. Rex Printing Company Ltd

02 03 04 05 06    10 9 8 7 6 5 4 3 2 1

For a complete list of titles available from Osprey Publishing
please contact:

Osprey Direct UK, PO Box 140,
Wellingborough, Northants, NN8 4ZA, UK
Email: info@ospreydirect.co.uk

Osprey Direct USA,
c/o Motorbooks International, PO Box 1,
Osceola, WI 54020-0001, USA.
Email: info@ospreydirectusa.com

**www.ospreypublishing.com**

This book is one of four volumes on the First World War in the
Osprey Essential Histories series

# Contents

Introduction    7

Chronology    9

Warring sides
Russia, Germany and Austria-Hungary    11

The fighting
From war to revolution    19

Portrait of a soldier
A trooper, an ensign and a sergeant    69

The world around war
The last days of Tsarist Russia    76

Portrait of a civilian
'Living on cereals and porridge'    81

How the war ended
The Bolsheviks seize power    84

Conclusion and consequences
The emergence of a superpower    90

Further reading    93

Index    94

# Introduction

That Russia, the most autocratically ruled of all the empires involved in the First World War, should in 1914 find itself aligned with the relatively democratic British and French Empires against the other autocracies of Germany, Austria-Hungary and Ottoman Turkey was neither inevitable nor accidental. Russia joined Britain and France to secure Greek independence from Ottoman rule in 1829, but for most of the next 80 years Britain and Russia were arch rivals, coming close to war several times, and actually going to war once, in the Crimea in 1853–56. The British and French supported Turkey then, mainly to thwart Russia's designs on the Turkish Straits, control over which would have placed it across the main route to their possessions in the Asia-Pacific region.

Temporarily frustrated there, Russia sought expansion on land to the south and east. It annexed the independent Khanates of central Asia, and combined them with land taken from China into the Governorates of the Steppe (now Kazakhstan) and Turkestan (now Turkmenistan, Uzbekistan, Kyrgyzstan and Tajikistan). Its southward expansion brought it close to the borders of British India, and increased their rivalry, the British fearing Russian invasion of India, the Russians British expansion into central Asia, and both contending for control over Iran, Afghanistan and Tibet.

In the east, Russia gained vast territories in the Amur valley and on the Pacific coast at China's expense, then sought hegemony over Manchuria and Korea. However, its ambitions collided there with those of Japan, which emerged in 1868 from over two centuries of isolation to adopt a European modernisation model complete with imperialism. Russia's defeats on land and sea in the Russo-Japanese War of 1904–05 led to nation-wide anti-regime disturbances in 1905. The Tsar sent in the police and Cossacks, established a Parliament, the Duma, but gave it no executive powers, and turned his attention back to Europe.

Expansion in Asia had never precluded continued Russian interest in the fellow-Slavs (Serbs, Croats, Slovenes, Bulgars, Czechs, Slovaks, Ruthenians, Poles) and Orthodox co-religionists (Serbs, Romanians, Bulgars) under Muslim Turkish or Catholic Austro-Hungarian control, where Russia could present itself as 'big brother'. In 1877–78 its victory over Ottoman Turkey ensured the independence of Romania, Serbia and Bulgaria; but British diplomacy again frustrated Russia's aim of controlling the Turkish Straits. That this remained an objective would be shown in 1915, when Russia secured British and French consent to including annexation of the Straits and the land on both shores, including the Ottoman capital, Constantinople (Istanbul), among its war aims.

The Triple Alliance Treaty between Germany, Austria-Hungary and Italy went through five versions, in 1882, 1887, 1891, 1902 and 1912. All five obliged the signatories to go to war if France attacked Germany or Italy, or if two or more Great Powers attacked any of them. The last four were also implicitly anti-Russian in their references to maintaining 'as far as possible' the status quo in 'the Orient', specified as 'the Ottoman coasts and islands in the Adriatic and Aegean' and, in an accompanying Austro-Italian Treaty of 1887, also 'the Balkans'. The third renewal, in May 1891, additionally mentioned the possibility of seeking British accession to the articles dealing with the Orient.

This prompted the French and Russian governments to reach in August 1891 a secret 'understanding on the measures whose immediate and simultaneous adoption would be imposed on the two governments by a threat of aggression against either. In August 1892 their General Staffs composed a secret Draft Military Convention. If Germany attacked either France or Russia, if Italy supported by Germany attacked France, or if Austria-Hungary supported by Germany attacked Russia, each would employ 'all her available forces to the full, with all speed, so that Germany may have to fight at the same time on the East and on the West', and neither would make peace separately. Russia was slow to accept the convention, but did so in December 1893. In 1912 this was supplemented by a Naval Convention, to cover 'every eventuality where the alliance contemplates and stipulates combined action of the land armies'. The Triple Alliance riposted in 1913 with a Naval Convention that even listed the ships each would deploy in the Mediterranean.

The Franco-Russian Conventions stipulated regular discussions between the General Staffs. These became especially frequent from 1911, and the French insistently advocated that the simultaneous offensives begin on the fifteenth day of mobilisation. This was feasible for France,

but Russia needed 40 days to mobilise, and at most only one-third of those mobilised could be on the Russo-German border in 15 days. Russia nevertheless accepted the French proposal, but undertook only to invade East Prussia, not to strike directly towards Berlin, as the French urged. In a war that made a bonfire of treaties and conventions, Russia's attempts to fulfil its obligations to France would be noteworthy, but would bring it military disaster in each year of the war.

In 1907, recognising Germany as a greater threat to both than either was to the other, Russia and Britain settled their differences in Iran, Afghanistan and Tibet. In Iran each defined a sphere of influence adjacent to its imperial borders in Transcaucasus and India, with an Iranian-controlled buffer zone between them. Russia acknowledged Afghanistan as 'outside the Russian sphere of influence', and Britain undertook not to occupy or annex any part of it. Both agreed to stay out of Tibet, and to respect China's suzerainty. Neither undertook any obligation to support the other in war; so the alliance with France remained central to Russia's military planning, and disrupting it central to Germany's.

# Chronology

1914  **28 June**  Archduke Franz Ferdinand of Austria assassinated in Sarajevo
**25 July**  Austria-Hungary declares mobilisation against Serbia
**28 July**  Austria-Hungary declares war on Serbia
**30 July**  Russia decrees full mobilisation
**1 August**  Germany declares war on Russia
**3 August**  Germany declares war on France; Austria-Hungary declares war on Russia; France asks Russia to attack Germany
**12–13 August**  Russia invades East Prussia
**17 August**  Battle of Gumbinnen
**20 August**  Battle of Stallupönen
**25–27 August**  Battle of Komarów
**27–31 August**  Battle of Tannenberg
**3 September**  Battle of Lemberg
**7–17 September**  Battle of the Mazurian Lakes
**11 September**  Battle of Grodek
**19–30 October**  First Battle of Warsaw
**7–17 November**  Second Battle of Warsaw
**11–12 November**  Battle of Wloclawek
**13–16 November**  Battle of Kutno
**19–25 November**  Battle of Lódz
**6–12 December**  Battle of Limanowa-Lapanów
**8 December**  Austrian Third Army retakes Carpathian passes
**30 December**  Battle of Sarikamis begins

1915  **17 January**  Russians finish mopping-up operations at Sarikamis
**22 March**  Russians capture Przemysl, taking 100,000 prisoners
**2–10 May**  Battle of Gorlice-Tarnów

**9–10 May**  Battle of Sanok
**13–18 May**  Battle of Jaroslaw
**20–22 May**  Austrians retake Lemberg
**July**  Russians withdraw from Galicia
**5 August**  Third Battle of Warsaw; Germans take Warsaw
**7 August**  Tsar appoints himself Commander-in-Chief
**September**  Zimmerwald Conference of Socialist International; Germans capture Vilnius
**October**  Battle of Dunaburg

1916  **17 January**  Battle of Köprüköy; Russians advance on Erzerum
**7 February**  Russians take Hinis
**11–16 February**  Battle of Erzerum; Russians take Erzerum and Mus
**18 March**  Unsuccessful Russian Vilnius offensive begins; ends 14 April
**April**  Kienthal Conference of Socialist International
**4 June**  Opening of Brusilov's offensive
**3–9 July**  Unsuccessful offensive by Russian West Front
**28 July**  Opening of second phase of Brusilov's offensive
**27 August**  Romania declares war on Austria-Hungary, invades Transylvania
**6 September**  Romanians complete occupation of Transylvania
**19 September**  German-led forces invade Transylvania
**3 October**  German victories in Transylvania and Dobrudja
**10 October**  Tsar terminates Brusilov's offensive
**16–17 October**  Final unsuccessful Russian effort to take Vladimir-Volynski

1917   **February** Cold weather disrupts food
and fuel supplies to Russian cities
**8–12 March** Food riots in Petrograd;
garrison troops mutiny
**12 March** Provisional Government
and Petrograd Soviet formed
**14 March** Petrograd Soviet Order
No. 1 claims control over garrison
**15 March** Tsar abdicates
**21 March** Tsar and family arrested
**16 April** Lenin arrives in Petrograd
**16 May** Kerensky becomes Minister
of War
**22 May** Kerensky appoints Brusilov
Commander-in-Chief
**18 June** Russian South-West Front
offensive begins
**2 July** Russian South-West Front
offensive ends
**8 July** Central Powers counter-attack;
South-West Front retires to river Seret
**10 July** North and West Front troops
refuse to attack
**13 July** Kornilov replaces Brusilov,
calls off offensives

**27 August** Failure of Kornilov's
attempt to seize power
**1–5 September** German Riga
campaign
**7 November** Bolsheviks seize
power
**8 November** Lenin proposes peace:
'no annexations and no indemnities'
**10 December** Armistice between
Romania and Central Powers
**17 December** Armistice between
Russia and Central Powers
**22 December** Russo-German peace
negotiations begin at Brest-Litovsk

1918   **9 February** Germany signs separate
peace with Ukraine
**16 February** Trotsky ends
negotiations, declares 'Neither war
nor peace'
**19 February** Germans advance to
within 80 miles (130km) of
Petrograd
**3 March** Treaty of Brest-Litovsk;
Russia leaves the war

# Russia, Germany and Austria-Hungary

## Ambitions

Conflict between Slav and Teuton had a long history, but Russia and Germany had not fought each other in modern times. Kaiser Wilhelm II and Tsar Nicholas II were cousins (both were grandsons of Queen Victoria), and Wilhelm's expansionist ambitions were directed not against Russia, but towards acquiring an overseas empire and challenging British hegemony at sea. He cultivated Nicholas as a potential ally or at least benevolent neutral, and to that end played on Nicholas' anti-British feelings, which were considerable, notwithstanding that King Edward VII was their uncle, and his successor, George V, their cousin.

Nicholas was convinced that without the Anglo-Japanese alliance of 1902 Japan would not have dared challenge Russia. In the war of 1904–05 Russia was soundly beaten on land by the German-trained and largely German-equipped Japanese army, but most humiliating of all was the navy's virtual annihilation by Admiral Togo's British-built and British-trained fleet. Wilhelm encouraged Nicholas' ambition to gain control of the Turkish Straits, assuming that the British would automatically oppose this. He was apparently unaware that in 1895 the British government had decided its communications with its Asian dependencies were secure enough that it was no longer vital to keep Russia out of the Mediterranean.

In 1905 Wilhelm even induced Nicholas to sign a treaty of alliance. This would have destroyed the more important alliance with France and prospects for French investment, so Nicholas' foreign minister, Lamsdorf, persuaded him to renounce it. Wilhelm continued cultivating Nicholas, but so did the British, ultimately with more success. The Anglo-Russian Convention of 1907 –

apparently, like the Anglo-French Entente of 1904, only a settlement of potential colonial squabbles – did not mention Germany, but was a sign that both empires saw Germany as a threat. However, neither undertook to go to war in support of the other.

Russia's size and population (in 1914 about 167 million, versus Germany's 65 million and Austria-Hungary's 51 million) rooted the idea that it was an inexhaustible manpower reservoir ('the Russian steamroller') among allies and enemies alike. But the true position was different. Profligate and inefficient use of manpower was endemic in industry and agriculture. Mass

Tsar Nicholas II, Tsaritsa Alexandra and son, Alexey. (Edimedia, Paris)

illiteracy increased armed forces' training problems, and the low level of mechanisation engendered not only low labour productivity but also low military 'teeth to tail' ratios. To maintain one Russian front-line soldier required two in rear services, compared to one in the rear for two at the front in the German and French armies. And large sections of the population were exempt from conscription.

All four empires on the Eastern Front were autocracies, but the Tsar had more absolute power than his counterparts in Berlin, Vienna and Constantinople. He appointed all government ministers, and they were answerable only to him. Moreover, Nicholas II had come to the throne in 1894 eager but untrained to rule – his father, Alexander III, planned to begin preparing him at the age of 30, but died four years too soon. Nicholas' German wife, Alexandra, was equally eager for power, but equally untrained, and her political views were reactionary by any standards. Had either been an outstanding individual, or Russia a constitutional monarchy, their shortcomings might have mattered less, but they were rather unexceptional people given exceptional powers; and as devoted parents, their main concern was to keep the autocratic powers intact for their son, Alexey, to inherit. Unfortunately his inheritance included, through his mother, another of Queen Victoria's grandchildren, the haemophilia that monarch bequeathed to Europe's royal houses. From at the latest 1912 the dissolute monk Rasputin had more influence over Alexey's parents than the Duma or any Cabinet minister because of his reputation as a faith healer and his uncanny ability to relieve the pain Alexey suffered from knocks or bruises.

Geography increased the gulf between rulers and ruled in Russia. The capital, Peter the Great's 'window on Europe', was a West-oriented enclave, mostly the work of Italian architects, closer geographically and intellectually to the other European capitals than to its own provinces. Even its name, 'Petersburg' (the 'Saint' was a later affectation), was German, Russianised to 'Petrograd' only after the outbreak of war; its aristocrats often spoke better French than Russian, Baltic Germans held high governmental and military posts, and Nicholas and Alexandra communicated with each other mostly in English. About 75 per cent of their subjects were illiterate peasant tenant farmers.

Industry, though growing fast, had come late to Russia, and an industrial working class existed in only a few cities. Peasant discontent over land tenure was matched by industrial unrest over low wages and poor working conditions, which in summer 1914 had workers overturning tramcars and building barricades in the capital's main streets. But as war approached, patriotic fervour erupted, and when the Tsar appeared in Palace Square, the crowd fell to its knees. Mobilisation was accompanied by considerable disorder, looting and riots, but they were caused by reservists *en route* to their units – that is, by men who did not question their duty to serve. They were the

Grigoriy Rasputin, the dissolute monk whose influence over the Russian royal family helped bring down the regime. He is shown here seated between Colonel Loma and Prince Putianin. (Ann Ronan Picture Library)

Field-Marshal Conrad von Hötzendorff, Austrian Chief of Staff. (Ann Ronan Picture Library)

consequences of inadequate provision for feeding them, or of delays in paying allowances to wives and families, not signs of opposition to the war.

There were, nevertheless, numerous potential time bombs in the multinational Russian Empire, additional to political discontent. First, like its rulers, the empire was not especially Russian. In 1897 its first census showed that only 44.3 per cent of the population was 'Great Russian'. Only by adding Belorussia ('White Russia' – a reference to soil colour, not politics) and Ukraine ('Little Russia') could the 'Tsar of all the Russias' claim two-thirds of his subjects as Russian. Turkestan and Steppe Governorates were overwhelmingly Muslim, and there were also large Muslim populations in Transcaucasus and Tatarstan. Doubt about the wisdom of giving Muslims weapons and military training was the main reason for exempting them from conscription. The Ottoman Emperor was *ex officio* Caliph of Islam, empowered in

principle to proclaim any war a *Jihad* (Holy War), and he might do just that in a war with Russia.

Nationalism elsewhere in the empire, compounded by cultural and religious differences, was a growing problem. The Russian Orthodox Church was widely (and rightly) seen as an arm of the Russian state by the predominantly Lutheran Finns, Estonians and Latvians, Catholic Lithuanians and Poles, and Ukrainian Uniate Catholics, and all these retained strong religious and cultural links with Scandinavia, central or western Europe. The Georgians and Armenians had their own Orthodox churches, much older than Russia's, and not accountable to the Russian Synod. Finnish nationalism became enough of a problem in the pre-war decade for the army's Finnish regiments to be temporarily disbanded and conscription of Finns suspended. Poland,

## Russia in 1914

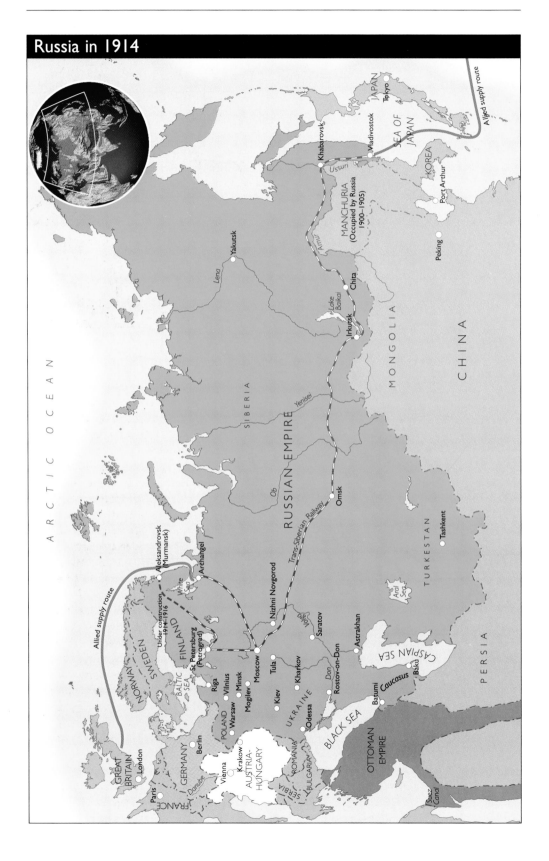

divided between Prussia, Austria-Hungary and Russia, would become the focus of a triangular contest of promises for post-war independence and reunification. Nor could Russia take Ukraine for granted; nationalism was resurgent there, among Orthodox as well as Uniates.

The uneasy Austro-Hungarian Dual Monarchy contained similar time bombs, because about 60 per cent of its subjects – Czechs, Slovaks, Poles, Ruthenians, Slovenes, Croats, and Bosnian Serbs – were Slavs. The army Chief of Staff, Conrad von Hötzendorff, had long been advocating preventive war on Serbia for encouraging unrest among the Hàbsburgs' South Slav subjects, and saw Franz Ferdinand's assassination as his opportunity. Russia inevitably lined up to support Slav Orthodox Serbia, and Germany to support Austria-Hungary against the Russian threat.

Germany had come late to empire building, and had a contiguous empire, like Russia, Austria-Hungary and Turkey, only in the sense that from 1871 the King of Prussia was also Emperor (Kaiser) of Germany. Its overseas dependencies were too small to contribute much to its war effort, and Entente, mainly British, sea power soon had them cut off or occupied. On the positive side, the Kingdoms of Prussia, Bavaria, Württemberg and Saxony, the several Grand Duchies, German Poland and Alsace-Lorraine contained no serious threat to unity; Alsace-Lorraine was not big enough to pose one, and most Poles saw Russia, not Germany, as the main obstacle to restoration of independence. Resentment of Prussian overlordship was widespread in the other German states, but did not affect their contribution to the Eastern Front.

Ottoman Turkey's army had performed poorly in 1912 against Greece, Serbia and Bulgaria, but was being reorganised and partly re-equipped by Germany. Its main roles in Germany's plans were to prevent the British and French using the Turkish Straits as a supply route to Russia, and to tie up some Russian forces in Transcaucasus. Turkey was effectively dragged into the war when

Enver Pasha, War Minister of the Ottoman Turkish Empire. (Ann Ronan Picture Library)

German Admiral Souchon, commanding its navy, bombarded Odessa on the night of 29–30 October 1914. Russia declared war on Turkey on 2 November.

Turkey's biggest potential time bomb was in its Arab dependencies, and affected the Eastern Front only in that Turkish troops fighting Arabs and their British or French patrons could not be used elsewhere. However, its Third Army confronted Russia's Army of the Caucasus in Eastern Anatolia, formerly part of Armenia. It had one specific war aim, the recovery of territory (Kars, Ardahan and Batum) annexed by Russia in 1878, and one much more grandiose objective, the ambition of Enver Pasha, Minister of War, to destroy the Army of the Caucasus, hoping thereby to kindle a revolt among Russia's overwhelmingly Turkic Muslim subjects in Transcaucasus and central Asia that would spread to Afghanistan and India.

Bulgaria and Romania joined the war on opposite sides in 1915 and 1916 respectively. Both did so in pursuit of territorial claims – Bulgaria against Serbia, Romania and Greece; Romania against Austro-Hungarian ruled Transylvania.

## Soldiers and equipment

The German army on the Eastern Front would always be outnumbered, but always be superior in training, leadership, supply and weaponry, built on a concept of the 'Nation in Arms' that was not yet fully accepted in 1914 by the other belligerents. Its core was the belief that conscripts, if well trained, equipped and led, would provide adequate front-line troops in larger numbers than those of other belligerents that used conscript reservists only for secondary or garrison duties. As in the West, Germany's Eastern Front infantry was backed by lavish artillery support, especially superior to Russia's in heavy guns and howitzers. Expecting only a short and mobile war, the German High Command had not yet fully grasped the importance of machine guns, but was much closer to doing so than the Russians, and equipped its troops with them on about eight times the Russian scale. With railways dominating land transport, the density and excellence of Germany's network gave it a great advantage in the speed with which it could supply its front-line troops, or transfer them between the Western and Eastern Fronts, or between north and south when the Austro-Hungarians needed support. Faced with an unexpected protracted war, Germany's industrial strength and communications enabled it to adapt better and faster than Russia or Austria-Hungary.

Prussia had once been described as an army possessing a state, rather than a state possessing an army. However, while Prussia undoubtedly provided the leadership and most formidable forces, those of the Kingdoms of Württemberg, Bavaria and Saxony, or Archduchies such as Baden, proved far more reliable than Slavs in Austria-Hungary's armies or non-Slavs in Russia's. Doubts about the reliability of French-speaking conscripts from Alsace-Lorraine generally precluded their use against France, but they fought well enough on the Eastern Front.

Austria-Hungary's annual intake of conscripts in the last pre-war years averaged 159,500, about 20 per cent lower proportional to its population than Germany, but nearly 50 per cent higher than Russia. However, only units from the empire's twin cores, the Ostmark (Austria) and Hungary, were completely reliable. Almost two-thirds of the empire's population shared ethnicity with countries across the borders, Italians in the west, Czechs, Slovaks, Ruthenians, Poles and Romanians in the east, Slovenes, Croats and Serbs in the south. Some attempt was made to keep ethnic kin apart, but there were not enough Austrians or Hungarians to man the Eastern Front without Slav troops, and they would prove unreliable against Russians, especially after mid-1916.

Parsimony was the rule in Austria-Hungary's defence spending. As late as 1911 it was less than a quarter of Germany's, and just over a quarter of Russia's. It rose with the adoption in that year of plans to increase the wartime army from 900,000 to 1.5 million, but remained comparatively low. In consequence, Austria-Hungary's armies were little better equipped than Russia's. Despite this, the Chief of Staff, Conrad, saw the assassination of Franz Ferdinand in June 1914 as an opportunity to flex military muscle that, unaided, proved insufficient even to beat Serbia.

Because it envisaged a short war, Germany saw no need to co-ordinate its Eastern Front operations with Austria-Hungary's, and contacts between the two General Staffs were almost completely in abeyance from 1896 to 1909. They resumed then at Conrad's insistence, but in 1914 the two countries still had no plans for joint action against Russia. At once differences in outlook emerged. With 70 of its initial 80 divisions engaged in the West, Germany envisaged only defence by the 10 divisions in the East for the 36–40 days that conquest of France was expected to take. Russia would then, it was expected, sue for peace, either at once or after briefly experiencing what 80 German divisions could do. Conrad, on the other hand, urged priority to attacking the southern flank (the 'Warsaw bulge') of Russian Poland. The Central Powers never fully resolved the problem of priorities between East and West.

Russia's peacetime army, of 1,423,000, was intended to rise within six weeks to 4,538,000, and a subsequent wartime peak of 6.5 million. However, its conscription system, based on a law of 1874, amended only slightly in 1912, did not foresee the colossal casualties of industrialised warfare and granted widespread exemptions. Many non-Slavs, including all Muslims, were altogether exempt for perceived backwardness, remoteness, or fear of the dangers of arming them. Sole breadwinners or only sons were exempt in peacetime, and liable only for garrison or auxiliary service in war. No records were kept of them, or of men with elder brothers already serving, or of second breadwinners, also seldom conscripted in peacetime. Their availability for war depended on their willingness to serve and police diligence in finding the unwilling. The German equivalent, the Ersatz or 'substitute' reserve, was as fully documented as the primary reserve, and mobilised on the outbreak of war.

Equally misconceived was Russia's policy in regard to the 1.1 per cent of men with higher education. Teachers, doctors, or chemists were mostly not conscripted in peacetime, and graduates in other disciplines served only one to three years instead of four; the system thus forfeited most possibilities for turning suitable graduates into reserve officers. These privileges, accorded only to the highly educated, overwhelmingly the sons of the wealthy, not surprisingly helped condition the masses to see conscription as a burden, not a civic duty, and to try to avoid it.

In Germany only about 2 per cent of men of military age could claim exemption for family or educational reasons, whereas in Russia 48 per cent could, and about half of those remained exempt even in wartime. The required numbers were achieved only by accepting the lowest physical standards in Europe. In Germany 37 per cent of conscripts were rejected on medical grounds, in Russia only 17 per cent. This meant not only higher sickness rates in the field, but also a more rapid decline in available reservists. On average 3 per cent of German reservists, but over 4 per cent of Russians, were de-listed annually on medical grounds. This meant that after ten years 75 per cent of German, but only 66 per cent of Russian reservists were still available; and when the call-up extended to men aged over 37, Germany had more available than Russia.

In the last pre-war years Germany trained on average 280,000 conscripts annually, while Russia, with over two and a half times Germany's population, trained 335,000, only 20 per cent more than Germany. And the average Russian conscript was of lower physical and much lower educational standards than his German counterpart, as well as less well trained and equipped. In most armies, non-commissioned and warrant officers provide much of a unit's professional backbone. They averaged 12 per company in the German army, but only two in the Russian.

When it came to equipment, Russia did not lack inventive minds, but application of their ideas lagged far behind the other principal belligerents. Only one plant, the Petrograd Arsenal, could make field guns, and only five others could repair them. When the armed forces expanded to wartime levels, artillery shortages at once became, and remained, endemic.

Machine guns were in equally short supply. In 1914 Russia had just over 4,100 (less than one per infantry battalion), and only the Tula Arsenal manufactured them. Contracts were placed with private firms, and attempts made to place orders abroad; but the other belligerents had already filled the foreign producers' order books, and as late as 1916 Russia's armies had only one-eighth of the machine guns they needed.

But the most acute shortage was in rifles and rifle ammunition, where requirements were underestimated by over one-third. There was a deficiency of 350,000 rifles at the outbreak of war, and by the end of 1914 recruits were commonly arriving unarmed at the front, some to be sent back, others sent into battle unarmed and told to take rifles from dead comrades. With a monthly need

Part of the Russian women's battalion in training. They were rounded up without fighting at the Winter Palace and told to go home. (Ann Ronan Picture Library)

for 200,000 rifles, production averaged 71,000 in 1915, and rose in 1916 only to 111,000.

In 1914 only three factories in Russia produced rifle ammunition. Monthly production, though trebled, remained only half of requirements throughout 1915, and not till April 1916 was it decided to build an additional manufacturing plant. By then the ammunition shortage was less acute, but only because the armies had only two-thirds of the rifles they needed. Meanwhile they had suffered a series of defeats, had enormous numbers of men captured, and lost large tracts of territory.

All First World War armies depended heavily on horses. Apart from cavalry (of which they all had more than they could use

on battlefields dominated by machine guns, trenches and barbed wire), artillery and field kitchens were horse-drawn, as were the carts that carried supplies from railheads to the front line. Horse fodder was usually the largest single item of supply, and the need to transport so much of it was an important factor in overloading the Russian railways.

Turkey's army was directly engaged against Russia only in Eastern Anatolia. The head of the German military mission, General Liman von Sanders, had great power over the army through its German Chief of Staff, General Bronsart von Schellendorf; a German Admiral, Souchon, commanded the navy and German staff officers occupied many senior positions. Their influence was, however, limited by War Minister Enver Pasha, who, as mentioned above, envisaged a much more ambitious role for Turkey's 36 divisions than Germany required of them.

# From war to revolution

On 30 July 1914, Russia began mobilisation. Only six days later the French ambassador 'entreated' the Tsar to attack immediately to relieve the pressure on the French army. Invasion of East Prussia by General Rennenkampf's First and General Samsonov's Second Army was hastily arranged. They outnumbered the 10 divisions of the German Eighth Army (General von Prittwitz und Gaffron) by about two to one, so the Germans planned holding actions in Mazuria, followed if need be by withdrawal to the strongly fortified lower Vistula river line, there to await

Grand Duke Nikolay, Russian Commander-in-Chief, 1914–15. (Ann Ronan Picture Library)

reinforcement by the conquerors of France. Russia's prospects were not enhanced when the Commander-in-Chief, Grand Duke Nikolay, responded on 8 August to more French pleas for help by taking two infantry corps from Rennenkampf for the attack towards Berlin that the French wanted.

## Russian invasion of East Prussia, August–September 1914

The Russians entered East Prussia on 12–13 August. At Stallupönen (17 August) and Gumbinnen (20 August) the First Army pushed the Germans back, placing East Prussia's capital, Königsberg (now Kaliningrad), in danger. Prittwitz, a court favourite rather than a good professional, panicked, so on 22 August Moltke replaced him and his Chief of Staff by Generals Hindenburg and Ludendorff. They arrived the next day, to begin the war's most formidable strategic partnership.

They inherited a critical but not hopeless situation. Rennenkampf's supplies were running short, and he could not use East Prussia's railways to resupply because the Germans had removed the rolling stock, and Russia's was of different gauge. When the Germans retreated after Gumbinnen he did not pursue them, but waited for two days for supplies to catch up. And when he did move, on 23 August, he gave avoiding a German flank attack priority over supporting the Second Army, continuing west towards Königsberg instead of turning south to meet Samsonov.

The Second Army had communication and supply problems, and was being imprudently urged on by the Front (Army Group) Commander, General Zhilinsky, over sandy soil that made progress difficult for

ABOVE Generals Hindenburg and Ludendorff, the dominant German command team in the east, later also in the west. (Edimedia, Paris)

RIGHT Some of the Russians captured at Tannenberg. The Germans claimed 92,000, the Russians admitted 60,000. (Ann Ronan Picture Library)

infantry and even harder for draft horses. The Russians made much use of radio, sending messages in plain text or a simple cipher that was easily broken. On 25 August the Germans intercepted two plain text messages, one by Rennenkampf, giving the distances his troops were to march on the next day, the other from Samsonov with orders for pursuing an enemy he believed to be in full retreat. They showed that the First Army would not be coming to meet the Second, and were such a gift that some wondered if they were a trap. However, the Eighth Army's Chief of Operations, Colonel Hoffman, had been an observer in the Russo-Japanese War and knew that Samsonov had suffered a defeat there because Rennenkampf had failed to support him, and that they had come publicly to

Colonel (later General) Hoffman, Chief of Operations of the German Eighth Army in 1914. (Ann Ronan Picture Library)

blows over it. Hoffman claimed thereafter that this knowledge convinced him mutual dislike would prevent them co-operating, and that the messages were genuine. However that may be, he acted on them, and was proved right. Leaving two divisions facing Rennenkampf, the Eighth Army hurled the other eight against Samsonov. Over 27–31 August his army was trapped; 18,000 were killed and 92,000 captured; on 29 August Samsonov shot himself.

The Germans named the battle after nearby Tannenberg, then turned on Rennenkampf, and in the Battle of the Masurian Lakes (7–17 September 1914) drove him out of East Prussia. His army did not disintegrate, but 45,000 were captured, and General Pflug's Tenth Army, on his left, also had to withdraw. By the end of September the Russians were back along the river

Niemen, minus over 250,000 dead, wounded or captured. Their sacrifice did, however, help France to survive. Five German divisions, rushed from the west in response to Prittwitz's panicky reports, arrived only after Tannenberg had shown they were not needed. They were immediately returned west, but arrived too late for the Battle of the Marne. Colonel Dupont, Head of French Intelligence, later said of the Russians that 'their débâcle was one of the elements of our victory'.

## Russian offensive in Galicia, August–September 1914

While Samsonov and Rennenkampf were heading into disaster, other Russian armies were trundling into Galicia (Austrian Poland). The 'Warsaw bulge' laid Galicia open to invasion from the northern as well as from the eastern, Ukrainian, side; Austria-Hungary's heterogeneous armies were

## The battle of Tannenberg and the battle of the Masurian Lakes

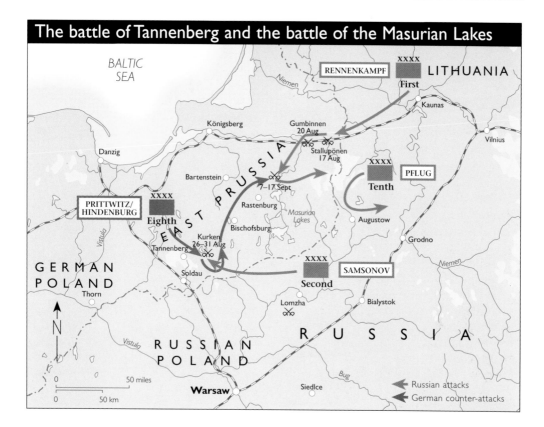

believed less formidable than the Kaiser's, and some Russian generals favoured knocking out Austria-Hungary before seriously tackling Germany.

Stavka (Russian GHQ) planned to take the Austrians in flank and rear by attacking south from the 'bulge' with the Fourth Army (General Evert), while the Third and Eighth (Generals Ruzhsky and Brusilov) advanced into Eastern Galicia. However, Conrad expected Russia's slow mobilisation to give him numerical superiority until late August, and was preparing to attack the 'bulge'.

Strategically each side stood to lose, as both proposed to attack forces that greatly outnumbered them. But misfortune for once came to Russia's aid. Ninth Army (General Lechitsky), assigned to the intended drive on Berlin, was deployed along the Vistula between Warsaw and Krasnik, and

General Alexey Brusilov. In 1916 his South-West Front conducted Russia's most successful offensive of the entire war. (Ann Ronan Picture Library)

when the East Prussian disasters temporarily foreclosed the Berlin option, it was already deployed where it could be best used against the Austrians.

In Eastern Galicia, the Austrian Third Army (General Brudermann), along the Grula Lipa river, was intended only as flank guard for the First and Fourth Armies, and was assisted only by the lightly armed Kövess Group, deployed south and west of it. Conrad intended also to use the Second Army (General Böhm-Ermolli) here, but it was *en route* to Serbia when he belatedly realised that its departure left Galicia weak. He recalled it on 30 July, but railway congestion slowed its return; not until 25 August was it in position, east of Sambor.

The Austrians attacked General Plehve's Fifth Army on 26 August, and the ensuing Battle of Komarów proved disastrous for Brudermann. When Ruzhsky's and Brusilov's advance guards fell upon the Third Army, he did not realise that their main bodies were close behind. On the 26th he counter-attacked without co-ordinating the two infantry corps involved, or arranging artillery support for either, and was routed. Russian ponderousness saved the Austrians' front from collapse, but they lost 350,000 killed, wounded or captured (almost half their total force) and most of Austrian Poland, and had 150,000 troops isolated in the fortress of Przemysl. By 16 September they had withdrawn behind the Dunajec river.

The Russian victory illustrated a dilemma that would plague Stavka throughout the war. German forces were closer than Austro-Hungarian to Russia's vital centres, and Germany was the main enemy, while Austria-Hungary's weaker forces could be contained or beaten with a relatively small proportion of Russia's, and the rest used against Germany. But it was also arguable that Germany could not survive alone, so

there were two schools of thought among Russia's generals, one giving priority to Germany, the other to the 'soft underbelly', Austria-Hungary.

On the German side, there was a tussle between 'Eastern' and 'Western' strategies. Moltke's plan staked everything on overrunning France before Russia completed mobilisation, and when it miscarried the Kaiser replaced him on 14 September with the Prussian War Minister, General von Falkenhayn. He had to work out how to fight a completely unforeseen protracted war, and his most immediate problem was settling priorities.

The fighting in Galicia had highlighted Austria-Hungary's shortcomings, while that in East Prussia demonstrated Russia's. To dig in on a defensible line in France and send most troops east to knock out Russia was an option. Falkenhayn, however, believed the Russians could avoid decisive battles by retreating, and victory must be sought in France, where the defenders had less room to trade space for time, and where the British, Germany's main enemy in his view, were involved.

Falkenhayn endorsed Moltke's belief that Germany must bolster the Austrian front, but without transferring forces from the west. On 16 September he approved

General von Falkenhayn, Prussian Minister of War, German Army Chief of Staff, September 1914–August 1916. He believed the Eastern Front secondary, but in 1916–17 commanded an army in the conquest of Romania. (Ann Ronan Picture Library)

Ludendorff's proposal to move most of the Eighth Army south to Silesia, to form a 'new', Ninth Army, commanded by Hindenburg. Ludendorff, its Chief of Staff, met Conrad on 18 September to discuss further action. Conrad resisted putting Austro-Hungarian troops under German command, and Ludendorff did not press him. He realised the Austrians needed a breathing space that only the Ninth Army could provide, and had already issued appropriate orders before going to meet Conrad. The Ninth Army began advancing north-east on 29 September, aiming to push the Russians back to the upper Vistula between Warsaw and Ivangorod (now Deblin) and draw Russian forces off from the Austrians, who would then, he hoped, resume their offensive.

## Battles of Warsaw, October–November 1914

Stavka knew by 23 September that German forces were in Galicia, and the Grand Duke laid a trap, switching all bar the Eighth and Third Armies to the German front. The Second and Fifth were sent north to the Vistula between Sandomierz and Warsaw, the First south from the Niemen to Warsaw, and the Tenth prepared a diversion on the Niemen. The Germans would be allowed to advance to the Vistula, then the First Army, plus most of the Second and Fifth, would attack their left flank south of Warsaw. The Germans did not discover the moves, assumed the Russians would attack the Austrians, and diverted three corps to meet the expected threat. In East Prussia, the Tenth Army advanced on 29 September, but had been halted by 5 October, and played no part in the main battle.

The Austrians realised by 4 October that they faced only a screening force, so they advanced to the river San, and relieved Przemysl on the 9th. Russian resistance then stiffened, and the Austrians were stopped. Belated realisation that the main Russian force was at least 30 miles (48km) further

Field-Marshal von Mackensen, commanded corps and armies in major battles in Russian Poland, Galicia and Romania. (Ann Ronan Picture Library)

north than expected forced Ludendorff to regroup. On 9 October an intercepted Russian radio message disclosed that seven Russian corps would be in the Warsaw area by 11 October, the day on which Mackensen, commanding IX Army's left flank, was supposed to capture Warsaw with only two corps.

On 10 October a copy of the Russian plan found on a dead officer showed Ludendorff that not only was the Ninth Army's left flank threatened from the Warsaw area, its right was also imperilled by the Russian Fourth and Ninth Armies, from bridgeheads on the west bank of the Vistula. On 11 October he ordered Mackensen to prepare for retreat. Falkenhayn spared only one corps from the west, where the First Battle of Ypres was imminent, and sent it to protect East Prussia; so relieving the pressure on the Ninth Army depended on the Austrians resuming the offensive on the San. Conrad, however, refused to do so, and rejected

General Alexeyev, Russian Army Chief of Staff, August 1915–mid-1917. (Ann Ronan Picture Library)

Ludendorff's alternative request to rush troops north to help Mackensen. The Kaiser appealed to Emperor Franz Josef; he upheld Conrad's refusal, but the Austrians took over the German Guard Reserve Corps' front at Ivangorod, freeing its two divisions to go north.

The Russians were now very strongly placed, with the Second Army west of Warsaw, and the Fifth in the city, preparing to pounce on Mackensen. On the 19th he began withdrawing, and a week later Ludendorff ordered a full-speed retreat of about 60 miles (100km) to a line between Kielce and Radom, to avoid being encircled. Preserving German forces now took precedence over helping allies, so the Austrians were left to their own devices, and their First Army also had to withdraw hastily, to prevent encirclement by the Russian Fourth and Ninth Armies. By the end of October the Russians had outrun their supplies, and the First Battle of Warsaw

ended. The Germans had lost all their initial gains, the Austrians rather more, and Przemysl was again isolated. Mackensen had evaded the Grand Duke's trap, but on the whole the Russians had had the better of it.

Inspired by this, the Grand Duke resumed planning a direct advance to Berlin. By early November nine armies stood in Russian Poland, a 'spearhead' of the Second, Fifth, Fourth and Ninth in the Vistula bend, with the Tenth and First protecting their right flank and the Third, Eleventh and Eighth their left. With seven-eighths of Germany's forces still on the Western Front, this concentration of more than 60 divisions, barely 300 miles (480km) from Berlin, clearly had great potential.

However, the South-West Front's commander, Ivanov, advocated acting first against the Austro-Hungarians in Galicia, to remove their threat to the south flank of the 'spearhead'. His Chief of Staff, Alexeyev, proposed sending the Third, Fourth and Ninth Armies south against Kraków and the battered Austrian First Army. This would halve the 'spearhead', so the Grand Duke rejected it, but he compromised by leaving the Third Army on the river San, and removing the Ninth from 'spearhead' to flank guard, covering the Kraków direction.

The 'spearhead' nevertheless remained large, and the northern flank guard's two armies were also to attack – General Sievers' Tenth to re-invade East Prussia with 20 divisions, Rennenkampf's First to advance along the Vistula west of Warsaw with six. The three 'spearhead' armies – the Second (Scheidemann), the Fifth (Plehve) and the Fourth (Evert) – totalling 26 divisions, were to advance west, the Fourth into Silesia, the others on to the flank of the German Ninth Army, now commanded by Mackensen and deployed between Kalisz and Czestochowa.

## Battle of Lódz, November 1914

The retreating Germans had systematically destroyed roads and railways, and consequent supply problems meant the

# The battle of Lódz to the second battle of Warsaw

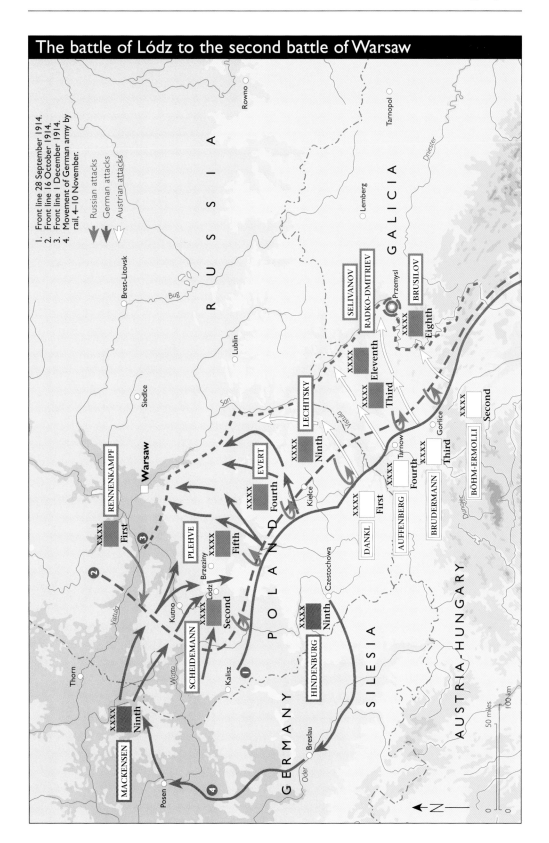

1. Front line 28 September 1914.
2. Front line 16 October 1914.
3. Front line 1 December 1914.
4. Movement of German army by rail, 4–10 November.

Russian attacks
German attacks
Austrian attacks

Russians' offensive could not start before
14 November. Eavesdropping on their radio
traffic gave Hindenburg, now *Oberost*
(Commander-in-Chief East), detailed
information on their intentions. On
3 November he took a bold decision, to
move the entire Ninth Army to Thorn (now
Torun), to attack south-eastwards into the
flanks of the Russian First and Second
Armies. His railways moved over 250,000
men in five days, and by 10 November the
Ninth Army, plus a corps from East Prussia,
was in position. Only four German divisions
remained to defend Silesia, but Conrad
reinforced them with the five of
Böhm-Ermolli's Second Army.

The Ninth Army attacked on
11 November. At Wloclawek on the 11th and
12th, it pushed V Siberian Corps aside, but
failed to destroy it. The Battle of Kutno
(13–16 November) was more decisive;
V Siberian and II Corps were badly mauled, a
40-mile (64km) gap opened between the First
and Second Armies, and three German
infantry and one cavalry corps poured south,
ending the Second Battle of Warsaw and
beginning the Battle of Lódz. By the 18th
Lódz was surrounded on all bar the south
side. By forced marches the Russian Second
Army brought up 500,000 troops in three
days, outnumbering the Germans by about
two to one, but arriving exhausted. For the
moment Lódz was saved, but it desperately
needed support. The nearest supporter was
the First Army, north of the city; but
Rennenkampf helped the Second Army there
as little as he had at Tannenberg.

That Russia narrowly avoided another
Tannenberg owed most to a broken promise
by Falkenhayn. A few days before
Hindenburg attacked, Falkenhayn, expecting
to win the First Battle of Ypres quickly,
promised to reinforce him by 24 November,
and Hindenburg planned his offensive
accordingly. But by the 18th First Ypres was
lost, Falkenhayn had no troops to spare and
Mackensen's Kutno victory had improved
Germany's position in the east as much as
Falkenhayn's defeat had worsened it in the
west. On the 18th Falkenhayn told

Hindenburg he would get no reinforcements;
he was so convinced of the Western Front's
primacy that he was pressuring Prime
Minister Bethmann Hollweg to seek peace
with Russia.

The Battle of Lódz was hard fought, and
fraught with miscalculations on both sides.
The Germans attacked on 19 November,
expecting an easy win, but the weather
suddenly turned cold with snow, favouring
the far more numerous defenders.
Nevertheless, General Scheffer's group
(XXV Corps, a cavalry force and the Guard
Division) advanced eastwards south of the
city, threatening to encircle it and the
Russian Second Army, and on the 21st one of
its brigades got within a mile (1.6km) of the
city centre. However, the defenders forced it
out, and by nightfall on the 21st Scheffer
had been halted. On the 22nd fresh Russian
divisions encircled his force at Brzeziny, and
ordered up trains to take away the expected
prisoners. However, Scheffer's boldness,
Russian lack of co-ordination and
Rennenkampf's inactivity combined to save
Scheffer's group. In three days it pushed over
20 miles (32km) through superior Russian
forces, taking with it not only 2,000
wounded, but 16,000 captured Russians and
64 Russian guns. Russian reconnaissance
mistook the march-column of prisoners for
Germans, and judged the enemy too strong
for their nearby forces to attack. Scheffer lost
half his force, but evaded the trap. Thus on
25 November ended the Battle of Lódz, again
aborting Russia's plan to drive to Berlin.

For the moment this gave the ascendancy
to the 'soft underbelly' school. To support
Mackensen, Conrad had attacked northwards
from Kraków on 18 November. However, the
Russians' unexpectedly strong resistance at
Lódz and on the Kraków front nullified
hopes of encircling them or sweeping them
back over the Vistula. Worse still, Conrad
had denuded his front from Kraków
eastwards, leaving its defence to the
11 divisions of General Boroevic's Third
Army and a few divisions hastily assembled
just south of Kraków. When Stavka realised
this, it at once launched Radko-Dmitriev's

Third and Brusilov's Eighth Armies, each with 10 divisions, against the entire front from Kraków east to the Bukovina.

Brusilov was very successful, advancing through the Carpathians almost on to the Hungarian Plain. But the Russians had co-ordination problems, because the North-West and South-West Fronts were diverging, their communications with each other and with Stavka at Siedlce were unreliable, and their experiences different. When their commanders met the Grand Duke on 29–30 November, Ruzhsky urged withdrawal almost all the way to the Vistula, to regroup, resupply, restore units battered at Lódz and await the German attack he believed imminent.

To do so would expose the South-West Front's northern flank, obliging it also to withdraw, and Ivanov rejected that. His forces had stopped the Austrians north of Kraków, made considerable gains south and east of it, and taken many prisoners, so he advocated another offensive. The Grand Duke vetoed Ruzhsky's proposal and accepted Ivanov's, for the Ninth Army to attack Kraków from the north and the Third from the south, each with four corps, while two corps of the Eighth Army maintained pressure in the Carpathians to prevent the Austrians reinforcing Kraków.

Conrad's four understrength armies between the Vistula and Carpathians were outnumbered by about two to one, and with Brusilov almost into Hungary the Dual Monarchy's heartland was directly threatened. So Conrad sent part of the Fourth Army (Archduke Josef Ferdinand) and one full-strength German division south from Kraków on to the Third Army's left flank, beginning the Battle of Limanowa-Lapanów. General Roth's four infantry and three cavalry divisions pushed forward on 3–6 December, forcing Radko-Dmitriev to halt and seek Brusilov's help. Brusilov sent VIII (General Orlov) and XXIV Corps (Tsurikov) into Roth's right flank, and the battle entered its second phase on 8 December, the Russians now trying to outflank Roth from the east.

They did not succeed, and the removal of two of Brusilov's corps to this battle left only one facing the entire Austrian Third Army. It also attacked on 8 December, and took the vital Dukla, Lupka and Uzhok passes, again thwarting Brusilov's advance on Hungary. The single corps retreated to north of the mountains, and this relieved the pressure on Roth, because Brusilov's two corps facing him had to withdraw in conformity. By 15 December the Russians had retreated to a shorter line along the Dunajec river. Some divisions had suffered 70 per cent losses, and the Austro-Hungarians had proved more hard nut than soft underbelly. That school therefore lost favour; though in fact Austria-Hungary never again did as well.

## Turkish front, winter 1914–15

Since Turkey and Russia were at war only from 2 November, with the severe Anatolian Highland winter beginning, Russia's Army of the Caucasus neither expected nor planned a major offensive, especially as Stavka had told its commander, Myslayevsky, to expect no reinforcements. However, I Corps (General Bergmann) tried a limited offensive on 2 November. The Turkish Third Army's commander, Hasan Izzet Pasha, enticed him forward for several days, then launched a counter-offensive threatening him with encirclement. Bergmann pulled back hastily, but lost about 40 per cent of his force before fighting died down on 16 November. Russia suffered other defeats on the northern sector, where irregulars ejected several garrisons, and for a time the port of Batum appeared vulnerable. The Grand Duke was sufficiently perturbed to ask for an Anglo-French 'demonstration' at the Straits to draw Turkish forces away. However, by 19 February 1915, when the Allies responded with the first attempt by warships to force a passage, the crisis in Transcaucasus was long past.

The main reason for this was that the November victories went to Enver Pasha's head. On 6 December he arrived in Erzerum, intent on destroying Russia's Caucasian Army and sparking revolts among Russia's Turkic subjects. His German advisers were

## The battle of Limanowa-Lapanów

Front line 15 December 1914
Front line 23 January 1915
Front line 15 March 1915
Front line 6 April 1915
Russian
German
Austrian

POLAND

0        50 miles
0        50 km

N

Vistula
San
Bug

Dunajec
Tarnow
RADKO-DMITRIEV
XXXX

Przemysl
○ Lemberg
Tarnopol ○

XXXX   Krakow
Lapanow ○
Fourth   Limanowa ○
ARCHDUKE
FERDINAND   Nowy Sacz

Third
XXXX
Gorlice
Eighth
Dukla Pass
Mezölaborcz ○   Lupka Pass

BRUSILOV

G A L I C I A

Dniester

Stanislav ○

Austro German
Force
ROTH   AUSTRIA-HUNGARY

Carpathian Mountains

Uzhok Pass
Verecke Pass
Wyszkow Pass

Prut

Czernowitz

---

privately sceptical, but failure would not affect the Eastern Front, while success would draw Russians away from it, so they did not try to dissuade him. Izzet Pasha and two of his corps commanders expressed doubts, so Enver dismissed them. The third corps commander said success was possible, given careful planning, winter clothing and extra rations, establishment of advance bases, and one additional corps. Enver kept him, but ignored his advice.

The offensive began on 22 December. It included an outflanking manoeuvre that required two divisions to spend two days traversing a barren high plateau with no warm clothing, no hot food and minimal rations. In a blizzard on the 24th one division lost 40 per cent of its men. Another spent a night in the open in a temperature of −36°F. Several hundred froze to death, thousands suffered frostbite and thousands more fled to the nearest villages for shelter; 50 per cent of the division was lost that night. Another lost one-third in a 19-hour march at nearly 10,000 feet (3050m) altitude.

The decisive Battle of Sarikamis began on 29 December, and the Russians finished mopping up on 17 January 1915. Of the 95,000 Turks engaged, 75,000 met death, wounding, frostbite, or captivity. Of 65,000 Russians, 16,000 were dead and 12,000 wounded or frost bitten.

## Winter campaigns, 1915

On 1 January Falkenhayn met Conrad and Ludendorff in Berlin. A week later, under pressure from the Kaiser and Bethmann Hollweg, he reluctantly agreed to send a few Eastern Front divisions to support Austria-Hungary in the Carpathians, and on 12 January he went to Hindenburg's headquarters at Posen (Poznan) to discuss his plans. On 23 January he agreed to give Hindenburg three newly raised corps that he would rather have sent west, and one transferred from the west because it was raised mostly in Lorraine, and not thought reliable for fighting the French. Three of these corps would form a new Tenth Army (Colonel-General von Eichhorn), take over the northern part of the front, from Gumbinnen to the Niemen river, and form the northern jaw of a pincer aimed at encircling the Russian Tenth Army (General Sievers). The Eighth Army (General Otto von Below), reinforced by the fourth new corps, would form the southern jaw of what was hoped would be a second Tannenberg.

The two armies totalled 15 infantry and two cavalry divisions, versus the 11 infantry and two and a half cavalry divisions of Russian Tenth, but Russian divisions had 16 battalions and German only 12, so they slightly outnumbered the Germans.

Russian trenches at Galicia. (Ann Ronan Picture Library)

However, the Germans had much more artillery, 924 light and 291 heavy guns, versus Sievers' 308 and 88, and a better supply network.

The Russians were again arguing about priorities. Ivanov cited the failures against the Germans as reasons for concentrating on Austria-Hungary, arguing that a convincing defeat would prompt Italy and Romania to invade it; it would then collapse, leaving Germany isolated. Ruzhsky argued that Germany was the main enemy, and force used against Austria-Hungary was wasted. The Grand Duke saw a flank attack from East Prussia as the greatest threat to his planned

drive on Berlin, and came down on Ruzhsky's side, giving Ivanov only one extra corps (Finnish XXII) and telling him not to attack. The bulk of reinforcements went to form a new Twelfth Army, under General Plehve, deployed south of the Tenth, to invade East Prussia from the south, by-passing the Masurian Lakes, while the Tenth invaded from the east.

Which side would be ready first depended on the railways. Here the Germans won hands down. On 5 February documents found on a dead German officer told the Russians that East Prussia had been reinforced, but they had no time to act on the information. Their offensive could not begin until 23 February, but the German

Destroyed fortifications at Przemysl. (Ann Ronan Picture Library)

Eighth Army attacked on the 7th, and the Tenth on the 8th. The weather was atrocious, varying from blizzards to daytime thaws, freezing again at night, so that even though both sides' troops had winter clothing, casualties from frostbite far outnumbered those of battle. The conditions favoured the defence because closing the trap required the Germans to move faster than the Russians.

Movement of any kind was difficult through snowdrifts and mud, fast movement impossible, and bringing supplies from railheads took up to 12 horses per cartload. But here, too, superior German organisation told; by 9 February most of the Russian artillery was out of ammunition, and under constant bombardment the Russian Tenth's north flank crumpled. By 17 February the Germans had taken over 60,000 prisoners, and had another 70,000 trapped in the Augustów forests. The east side cordon was

three-quarters of the Tenth Army's 396 guns. But the grander aim of forcing Russia to abandon the Vistula line had not been achieved, and the accompanying Austro-Hungarian offensive failed. However, the Russian public did not know Hindenburg's aim, or that he fell short of achieving it. They knew only that another army had been wiped out, and that soldiers' letters spoke of overwhelming German artillery bombardments, Russian guns silent for lack of shells, and infantry mown down or captured by the tens of thousands.

The Austro-Hungarian front offered Russia more cheer. Since mid-September it had the fortress of Przemysl, with over 100,000 defenders, under siege – though the length of siege reflected Russia's lack of heavy artillery. Ivanov stuck to his plan to invade Hungary through the Carpathians, while Conrad saw an attack from them as Austria-Hungary's contribution to forcing the Russians off the Vistula line.

So both planned winter offensives in the Eastern Carpathians. Terrain less suited to a winter campaign is hard to imagine. The mountains, though not very high, are steep sided, intersected by few passes and even fewer passable roads, and blocked by snow on most days, and by mud during the occasional thaws. Thousands of troops on both sides died of exposure that winter.

The Austrians moved first. On 23 January 1915, 20 divisions attacked at the Dukla, Lupka and Uzhok passes. Simultaneously the new 'German South Army' (mostly Austrian, but under a German general, von Linsingen) attacked the eastern Verecke and Wyszkow passes. The Eighth Army, with approximately equal strength, held the attacks, and they were called off on the 26th. Brusilov then attacked at the Dukla and Lupka passes, sowing havoc among Boroevic's Third Army, which in three weeks lost over 65,000 of its 100,000-plus manpower to battle or frostbite.

By mid-February the Russians had captured the important railway junction of Mezölaborcz, and were prevented from exploiting their success only by having to divert resources to counter General

too thin to stop some escaping, but about half were captured by the 22nd, and two days later another 10,000 surrendered at Przasnysz.

The Germans were now nearing exhaustion, and Russian counter-attacks in the last days of February prompted Hindenburg to end the offensive and pull back from the most exposed positions. By the end of March another 40,000 Russians had been captured, and the front was stable just east of the frontier. The Russians had lost 150,000 in prisoners alone, and

Winter 1914–15 in the Carpathians. (Edimedia, Paris)

Pflanzer-Baltin's advance towards the Dniestr river at the eastern end of the front. A second Austrian offensive from 27 February achieved only limited success in the Carpathians, but Linsingen and Pflanzer-Baltin succeeded by mid-March in forcing the Russians back across the Dniestr.

On 22 March the Russians captured Przemysl, taking 100,000 prisoners and freeing the Russian Eleventh Army for use elsewhere. Another Russian assault through the Carpathians began the same day, and by mid-April the Austrians were fortifying the Danube line between Vienna and Budapest, anticipating a Russian exodus on to the plain. But by then the Eighth Army had again run out of artillery ammunition, and German reinforcements helped stabilise the line. Most of Austria's regular officer cadre had by now been lost, and though the Russians were in no better case, their 'soft underbelly' advocates seemed triumphant.

## Breakthrough at Gorlice-Tarnów

However, Falkenhayn now had to look more to the east, because Austria-Hungary's reverses prompted Italian and Romanian hints that only territorial concessions could prevent their declaring war. Conrad and Falkenhayn opted to overawe them by crippling Russia's offensive power. They planned a surprise attack on the Russian Third Army over a 78-mile (125km) front between Tarnów in the north and the Lupka pass in the south. Its focal point was the city of Gorlice, and it went into history as Gorlice-Tarnów.

Falkenhayn took his decision on 9 April, and after discussion with Conrad eight German divisions received orders on the 15th to move secretly from the Western to the Eastern Front, to form a new Eleventh Army under Mackensen, deployed west of Gorlice. Conrad gave Mackensen control over the Austrian Fourth Army, on the Tarnów sector to his north, and the Third to

## The battle of Gorlice-Tarnów

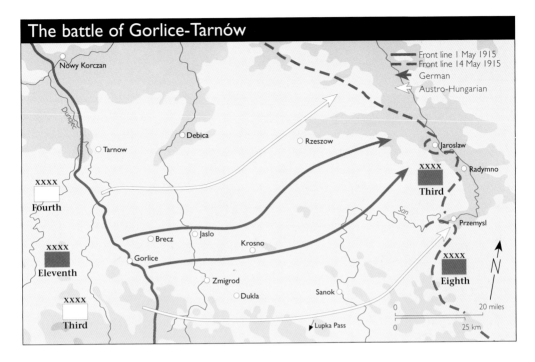

his south, covering the Dukla and Lupka passes. 'Army Group Mackensen', with 22 infantry and one cavalry divisions, faced 19 Russian divisions, all understrength and short of artillery. The Eleventh Army was to break through at Gorlice and force the Russian Third back to the river San, the Austrians providing flank support and attacking to roll back the Carpathian front.

The attack on 2 May achieved almost complete surprise. By 3 May Gorlice had been taken, and a 12-mile (19km) hole ripped in Radko-Dmitriev's line. Three of his divisions broke and fled, the rest were down to an average of only 1,000 men by evening on 4 May, and his only option was withdrawal behind the Vistula. Destruction of his centre uncovered the northern flanks of two of his corps in the Carpathians, but if they withdrew Brusilov would also have to pull back, aborting the invasion of Hungary yet again. On 5 May the Grand Duke vetoed withdrawal, but that same day further thrusts by the Austrian Third Army towards Lupka and the German Eleventh towards Sanok forced the Third Army into an unstoppable retreat. By 10 May, Radko-Dmitriev reported, it had 'bled to

death', and Ivanov ordered withdrawal from the Carpathians. The Grand Duke asked the British and French to attack urgently to draw off German forces, and to nudge Italy into the war, to draw off the Austrians.

Falkenhayn saw the victory of Gorlice-Tarnów as important enough to transfer the Supreme Command from the west to Silesia, and plan a joint Austro-German effort to cripple Russia permanently. A local success by the Russian Ninth Army, pushing Pflanzer-Baltin back from the Dniestr to the Prut, was the only bright spot for Russia, and too remote to affect matters in Galicia, where both the Third and Eighth Armies lost heavily in the Battle of Sanok (9–10 May). On the 16th, the German Eleventh Army reached the San, and forced a crossing in the five-day Battle of Jaroslaw. An attempted Russian counter-offensive between 15 and 22 May was unsuccessful.

Nor did Italy's declaration of war on Austria-Hungary on 25 May provide any immediate relief. Austrians began leaving for the Italian front only on 3 June, and Germans arrived to replace them. The Austrian Third Army was disbanded, its divisions shared between the Second and Fourth, and regrouped with the German Eleventh for a new venture – recapture of Lemberg (now Lviv), capital of Galicia.

## Russian retreat

By now Russian losses were soaring. In May alone, the South-West Front lost 412,000 killed, wounded or captured. Mackensen resumed his offensive on 12 June, and by the 17th had advanced to the line Rava Russkaya–Zolkiew, while the Austrian Second Army was closing on Lemberg.

The Vistula line, already threatened with outflanking from the north, was now also vulnerable from the south. There were insufficient guns, small arms and ammunition for a counter-offensive. Galicia would have to be abandoned, to shorten the line and free troops for a strategic reserve, so on 17 June the Grand Duke ordered a fighting retreat. It was 'to be deferred as long as possible', but events were moving fast. On 20 June loss of the Rava Russkaya–Zolkiew line bared Brusilov's right flank, so he ordered war stores evacuated from Lemberg and all forces in Galicia prepared to withdraw. The Battle of Lemberg began that day, with two of Brusilov's corps (VIII and XVIII) facing the numerically superior and fresher German XLI Reserve and Austro-Hungarian VI Corps. On the 22nd, the Austrians broke into the outskirts, and Brusilov avoided entrapment only by abandoning the city.

Gorlice-Tarnów and Lemberg, immediately followed by the Third Battle of Warsaw, were cumulatively even more disastrous for Russia than Tannenberg. Fifteen divisions were wiped out, and about 20 more reduced to skeletons. The retreat from Galicia left the Vistula line untenable, and it, too, was abandoned.

Warsaw fell on 5 August. The Grand Duke, like Kutuzov in 1812, had traded space for time. But the armies of 1812 were tiny compared to those of 1914–15, there was neither a continuous front line nor streams

of refugees, and the country, apart from the narrow belt traversed by the armies, was little affected. In 1915 the consequences of retreat were far greater.

The front-line troops' retreat from Poland was orderly. But ahead of them were over two and a half million refugees, forced to leave by

having their towns and villages burned under the Grand Duke's 'scorched earth' policy. The refugees were being dumped from trains in towns, some as far away as central Asia or Siberia, that were too gripped by shortages of food, fuel and accommodation to provide adequately for them. The impression this left

Russian 'scorched earth' policy. A burning Polish village. (AKG, Berlin)

on rear-service troops and the population was far worse than the purely military situation warranted. Apparently believing the army had cracked, Nicholas decreed draconian punishments for surrender, including cessation of allowances to families, and post-war exile to Siberia. These decrees merely reinforced the public's impression of disaster. The new War Minister, General Polivanov, told the Council of Ministers on 30 July, 'demoralisation, surrender and desertion are assuming huge proportions', and the Minister of Agriculture, Krivoshein, warned that 'the second great migration of peoples, staged by Stavka, will bring Russia to the abyss, revolution and ruin'.

The immediate consequence was the dismissal of the Grand Duke, for which Alexandra and Rasputin had long been lobbying. Alexandra suspected him of plotting to become Tsar, and saw his support for representative government as intended to undermine the autocracy. The retreat gave them the opportunity to pressure Nicholas. On 7 August, two days after Warsaw fell, Nicholas dismissed him and appointed himself Commander-in-Chief. The soldiers grieved, Ludendorff (later to say 'The Grand Duke was a great soldier and strategist') rejoiced. The Council of Ministers was aghast, believing Nicholas' action would now focus the nation's anger on himself. The generals were less upset, seeing him as a figurehead, with a professional Chief of Staff taking the important decisions. Nicholas' appointee, General Mikhail Vasilyevich Alexeyev, was highly respected by his colleagues, and with Polivanov in office, they believed that supply would never again be as bad. The British and French governments heaved sighs of relief, taking Nicholas' action as evidence that Russia meant to stay in the war.

The retreats continued and public anger mounted. The Falkenhayn–Conrad plan to cripple Russia permanently seemed to have succeeded, and as the autumn rains began, Falkenhayn started returning troops to the west. Yet Austria-Hungary was in little better state than Russia. It, too, had suffered supply shortages and immense casualties – over 800,000 in the Carpathian winter campaign alone, increased to 1,250,000 by the 1915 summer campaign. Only massive German reinforcement had saved the

Austrian front from collapse, and the Habsburgs had become satellites of the Hohenzollerns, with German generals such as Linsingen, Bothmer and Mackensen commanding Austrian forces, and German priorities determinant. The home front faced a food crisis nearly as bad as Russia's, for the same reason – the blockade added to unmechanised agriculture's difficulty in maintaining production when most of the able-bodied peasants had been conscripted. Conrad's last attempt at independent military action was an offensive in the Rovno area in September 1915, and it failed. So an energetic assault might break Austria-Hungary.

## Russian offensive in Turkey, winter 1915–16

After Sarikamis the Russo-Turkish front was quiet for almost a year, except for localised campaigns in Persian Azerbaijan in April and around Lake Van in May–June. The Turks were preoccupied with reorganisation, the Gallipoli campaign and 'ethnic cleansing' in Turkish Armenia, and the Russians could not contemplate an offensive because the Caucasus Army's needs had low priority compared to those of the Eastern Front proper. The situation began to change following the arrival of the Grand Duke Nikolay, whom the Tsar appointed Viceroy and Commander in the Caucasus in September. On the night of 19/20 December the Allies evacuated Gallipoli, and the Caucasus Army's Chief of Staff, General Yudenich, realised that this would free Turkish forces for use elsewhere, principally against his front. Secondly, Serbia's collapse in October and Bulgaria's entry into the war on Germany's side, had reopened the land route from Germany to Turkey. German weapons, especially artillery pieces, could now flow unimpeded to the Turks. Thirdly, Turkish supply routes and services were so inadequate that neither of these could happen quickly.

There was a 'window of opportunity' of several weeks for destroying the Turkish

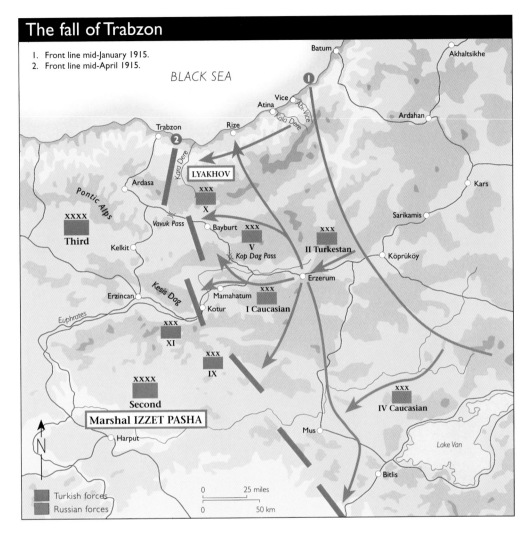

## The fall of Trabzon

1. Front line mid-January 1915.
2. Front line mid-April 1915.

BLACK SEA

Batum
Akhaltsikhe
Vice
Atina
Ardahan
Trabzon
Rize
Kars
Ardasa
LYAKHOV
Pontic Alps
XXX
X
Sarikamis
Third
Vavuk Pass
Bayburt  XXX
XXX
Köprüköy
Kelkit
V
II Turkestan
Kop Dag Pass
Erzincan
Erzurum
Mamahatum
XXX
Kotur    I Caucasian
Euphrates
XXX
XI
XXX
IX
XXX
IV Caucasian
Second
Marshal IZZET PASHA
Mus
Lake Van
Harput
Bitlis

Turkish forces
Russian forces

0        25 miles
0              50 km

Third Army, and there was another appeal for help from an ally. This time it came from the British in Mesopotamia (now Iraq), whose attempt to advance to Baghdad had been stopped at Ctesiphon. They had had to retreat, and since 7 December had been besieged in Kut al-Amara by Turkish forces in daily increasing numbers. The British therefore asked for a Russian attack in Anatolia, to draw some Turks away, and this gave the Grand Duke an additional reason to act quickly. He approved Yudenich's plan on 31 December, and the offensive began on 10 January 1916.

Yudenich assumed, correctly, that the Turks would not expect a Russian offensive in the depths of winter – the Third Army's

commander, Kamil Pasha, and Chief of Staff, a German, Major Guse, were both away. The Russians had 325,000 troops available, the Turks 78,000, and Russian supply services, which included 150 lorries, were superior to their Turkish equivalents. These were entirely dependent on beasts of burden, had few good roads and had been disrupted by deportation or worse of the Armenian conscripts who provided clerical and labour services in the Third Army, and of the Armenian farmers who provided much of its food. The Russians also controlled the sea, and had air superiority – the 20 aircraft of the Siberian Air Squadron.

Like Enver's 1914 plan, Yudenich's required the troops to march over high

mountain plateaux and ridges in blizzards and deep snow. But unlike Enver's troops, the Russians were adequately clad and fed, and carefully trained beforehand. The Turks chose to stand at Köprüköy, 40 miles (64km) east of Erzerum, and concentrated five divisions there, leaving only one to guard the south–north road from Bitlis, at the west end of Lake Van, to Erzerum, along which most of Erzerum's supplies came. The Russian 4th Caucasian Rifle Division marched over the high Cakirbaba ridge to split the Turkish defences on 14 January. Some 25,000 Turks were killed or captured, and the rest fled to Erzerum.

The fortifications of Erzerum comprised 15 forts with about 300 mostly obsolete guns. A ridge, over 9,600ft (2,900m) high, between the northern and central forts was presumed impassable, so was neither fortified nor occupied. The Russians moved on to it, but after an entire battalion froze to death they rotated troops so that most spent only a few hours there at a time. As the fort system could be adequately manned only by about twice the 40,000 defenders, it was to be attacked at several points, and simultaneously the town of Mus on the north–south road was to be captured, to block any Turkish reinforcements or supplies that might be on their way.

The assault began on 11 February, and four days later the Third Army abandoned Erzerum. The Russians entered the city the next morning, and captured Mus on the same day. Only about 25,000 Turks escaped; the Russians captured over 12,000, and 327 guns, at a cost of about 3,000 killed in battle or by exposure, 7,000 wounded and about 4,000 non-fatal frostbite cases.

The next phase of Yudenich's plan involved an advance along the Black Sea coast, and was noteworthy for skilfully conducted combined operations using shallow-draft barges to land troops, and the big guns of warships to provide the heavy artillery support that the army elsewhere

Victorious Russian cavalry entering Trabzon. (Ann Ronan Picture Library)

lacked. The Russian Black Sea Fleet (Admiral Eberhardt) had maritime supremacy, challenged only sporadically by two modern German warships (*Goeben* and *Breslau*) and one submarine (*U33*), and its main operating difficulty was the 450-mile distance from its main base, Sevastopol, and nearest subsidiary base, Novorossiisk.

Between 5 February and 6 March the Turkish Third Army was turned out of several defensive positions along the coast by a combination of naval bombardment and landings of troops behind them. The Russians halted about 30 miles (48km) east of Trabzon because of faulty intelligence reports that a large Turkish force was in the vicinity, but resumed the offensive on 14 April, and entered Trabzon on the 18th. The Turkish Second Army had been brought into the area in February as part of a German-devised plan for a south–north drive across the Russian lines of communication; but it managed no more than a temporary blockage of the Russian drive towards Erzincan.

# Brusilov offensive, June–August 1916

On the Eastern Front proper, neither allies nor enemies thought Russia capable of a major offensive in 1916, so Falkenhayn continued transferring troops to the west for his battle of attrition at Verdun. The Allies, too, resolved on a major Western Front offensive, on the Somme, to begin on 1 July, and sought limited Russian support, to inhibit German westward transfers. Stavka therefore ordered North and West Fronts (Generals Kuropatkin and Evert) to plan an offensive towards the important rail centre of Vilnius for some time in May. However, the Verdun battle, which began on 21 February, spurred more frantic French appeals for help, so the offensive was advanced to 1 March.

The North Front, along the Dvina river, comprised two armies (Fifth and Twelfth), the West Front five (First, Second, Third, Fourth and Tenth). One from each front was to attack, the Fifth to advance its right wing out of its Yakobshtadt (Jekabpils) bridgehead, the Second to advance north and south of Lake Narozh, to meet the Fifth, closing a pincer on the German XXI Corps, then advance to Vilnius. The Twelfth, Fifth and First Armies were to pin down German reserves. The West Front's assault force totalled 30 divisions, with about 400,000 men, on a 43-mile (70km) front.

The artillery support was modest by German standards, but Russia's heaviest yet. However, the prolonged concentration process was, as usual, detected, and the Germans reinforced beforehand. The 1 March deadline could not be met, for lack of rifles; so Stavka ordered the West Front to move on 18 March, and the North on the 21st.

On 17 March the spring thaw began unexpectedly early, turning the ground ahead of the Russians into an almost impassable quagmire. Nevertheless, the offensive proceeded. Despite unprecedented expenditure of shells, and disregard for casualties, the West Front failed utterly. In three weeks it took an area slightly more than 1 mile deep by 2 miles wide (1.6 × 3.2km), at the price of 70,000 killed, wounded or captured, and in one day, 14 April, the Germans retook it all.

On the North Front, General Gurko fared somewhat better, by attacking later (21 March), and desisting sooner (26 March). He committed only four of his eight divisions; they had over 28,000 casualties, more than one-third of their strength. Diversionary attacks south of Riga and west of Dvinsk neither prospered nor drew off Germans. The two Fronts' casualties totalled 110,000, but the main casualty was morale. This time immense efforts had been made to provide enough weapons and ammunition, but failure was again complete.

Stavka blamed the commanders for bad organisation, the artillery for not supporting the infantry, and the infantry for lacking dash. But the real culprit was Stavka's blithe insouciance in going ahead despite the thaw. Nor did the offensive draw off any Germans from Verdun. However, when Alexeyev

# The Brusilov offensive

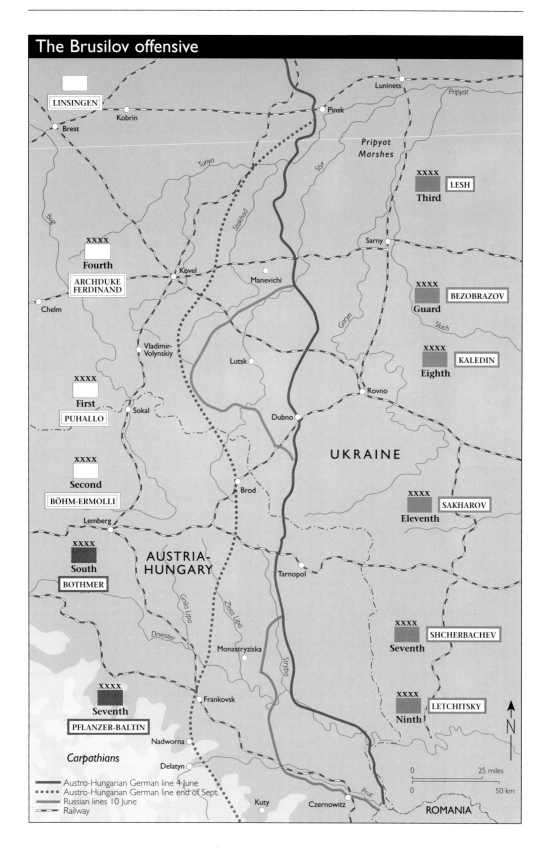

LINSINGEN

Brest    Kobrin    Pinsk    Luninets    Pripyat

Pripyat Marshes

XXXX    LESH
Third

XXXX
Fourth
ARCHDUKE
FERDINAND

Kovel    Manevichi    Sarny

Chelm

XXXX    BEZOBRAZOV
Guard

Sluch

Vladimir-
Volynskiy

XXXX
First
PUHALLO

Sokal    Lutsk

XXXX    KALEDIN
Eighth

Rovno

Dubno

UKRAINE

XXXX
Second
BÖHM-ERMOLLI

Brod

XXXX    SAKHAROV
Eleventh

Lemberg

XXXX
South
BOTHMER

AUSTRIA-
HUNGARY    Tarnopol

Gniła Lipa

Złota Lipa

Dniester

XXXX    SHCHERBACHEV
Seventh

Monastryziska

Serpa

XXXX
Seventh
PFLANZER-BALTIN    Frankovsk

XXXX    LETCHITSKY
Ninth

N

Nadworna

Carpathians    Delatyn

0        25 miles

0        50 km

Prut

——— Austro-Hungarian German line 4 June
••••• Austro-Hungarian German line end of Sept.
——— Russian lines 10 June
–•–•– Railway

Kuty    Czernowitz    ROMANIA

Bug    Turiya    Stokhod    Styr    Goryn

began to plan 1916's main operation – the offensive to support the Somme – he produced only an expanded version of it.

For supporting the Somme it did not matter whether German troops stayed in the east defending themselves or helping Austria-Hungary. But Alexeyev had no doubt that the major effort should be against Germany, and proposed a renewed attempt to recapture Vilnius using the West Front, supported by the North. The South-West Front would join in only after the West's advance had exposed the Austrians' left flank, and would receive no extra resources. Most of Stavka's artillery and infantry reserves would go to Evert, the rest to Kuropatkin.

The South-West Front's commander, Ivanov, had become chronically depressed, and was replaced by Brusilov at the end of March. On 14 April Nicholas summoned a Council of War at Mogilev, to consider Alexeyev's proposal. At the Council Kuropatkin predicted immense casualties, for lack of heavy artillery ammunition. War Minister Shuvayev and Head of Artillery Grand Duke Sergey confirmed that heavy shells would remain scarce, whereupon Evert endorsed Kuropatkin's objections, opposing any offensive until artillery supply improved.

At this point Brusilov sought permission to attack simultaneously with Evert and Kuropatkin, arguing that at worst he would improve their chances by pinning down enemy forces. Alexeyev agreed in principle, and Evert and Kuropatkin then grudgingly accepted his plan, with a provisional deadline in May.

The North and West Fronts' preparations followed the conventional pattern. A sector about 28 miles (45km) wide was chosen west of Molodechno, and 47 divisions assembled in it. The main force was General Ragoza's Fourth Army (22 infantry divisions), while south of it were Radkevich's Tenth (15 infantry and three cavalry), and the new Guard Army under Bezobrazov (four infantry and three cavalry). Ammunition dumps were established, roads improved, artillery and supplies brought in; and, as usual, German air reconnaissance and spies saw them come.

Since the front north from the Pripyat river to the Baltic was the nearer to Russia's and Germany's vital centres, all bar four German Eastern Front divisions were north of the Pripyat Marshes, and the preparations caused them no anxiety. The planned operation was orthodox and therefore predictable; they would have ample advance notice of its starting, and could withstand it.

Brusilov rejected the orthodox approach. Troop and supply concentrations and trench-digging could not be concealed, so he decided to confuse the Austrians by having all four armies dig trenches along their entire front, and each have all its corps attack somewhere. The main assault would be by General Kaledin's Eighth Army towards Kovel, where the north–south railway behind the enemy front crossed two west–east lines; but the Austrians could not extract this from a picture of frenzied activity everywhere. He deliberately violated the principle of 'concentration of force' to increase his chances of surprise.

His four armies (from north to south, the Eighth, Eleventh, Seventh and Ninth) occupied a front about 300 miles (480km) long, between the Pripyat Marshes and the Romanian frontier, with 36 infantry and 12.5 cavalry divisions, comparable to the 37 infantry and 9 cavalry (42 Austro-Hungarian, 4 German) divisions facing them. Brusilov's efficient combination of aerial reconnaissance and spies kept him better informed than the enemy about the forces facing him.

From north to south they were an 'Army-sized Group' under Linsingen, the Austrian Fourth (Archduke Josef Ferdinand) and Second (Böhm-Ermolli) Armies, the German Southern Army (despite its name, and its Bavarian commander, von Bothmer, it was mostly Austro-Hungarian) and the Austrian Seventh Army (Pflanzer-Baltin). More than half the Austro-Hungarian troops were Slavs, mostly better disposed towards Russians than towards their Austrian or Hungarian overlords. Since March 1916 Ludendorff had advocated a unified eastern command under Hindenburg, but the Austrians opposed publicising their subservience, so no such command yet existed; the front facing Brusilov was under the Austrian Archduke Friedrich.

Brusilov could not set an attack date until he knew that of the main offensive. On 20 April he ordered his armies to be ready any time after 11 May, but Evert's preparations proceeded so slowly that a co-ordinated offensive clearly could not begin until June. Then, as before, events elsewhere forced a change of plan.

On 15 May the Austrians attacked on the Italian front, and their initial successes prompted urgent Italian appeals for Russian help. Evert was still dragging his feet, but Brusilov's preparations were so advanced that on 24 May Alexeyev asked him if he could attack alone. Alexeyev can only have done this on the Tsar's orders, and like the responses to appeals by the French in 1914 and February 1916, and the British in 1915, it put fidelity to allies above Russia's own interest. Sending the South-West Front alone into action destroyed the entire concept of a co-ordinated offensive. Brusilov, attempting to retain it, offered to attack on 1 June, provided Evert attacked simultaneously, to prevent the Germans moving troops to his front. Alexeyev told him Evert could not attack before 14 June, and asked him to postpone his own offensive to 4 June. On being assured that there would be no further postponement, he agreed. However, late on 3 June Alexeyev telephoned, expressed grave doubts about Brusilov's plan and suggested postponement to regroup for an orthodox single blow. Brusilov refused and offered his resignation; Alexeyev, having covered himself and Stavka against possible failure, withdrew his suggestion.

When the offensive opened on 4 June, two questions were crucial. Did the Austrians know what to expect? How would the troops perform? The answer to the first soon became clear: they did not. The second had less simple answers. Most performed well, but there was a worrying desertion rate. Between 15 May and 1 July, 10,432 men deserted from the Seventh Army, 24,621 from the Eighth, 9,855 from the Ninth and 13,108 from the Eleventh. Thus, during three weeks of quiescence and four of a successful offensive, enough men for three full-strength divisions deserted.

The Eighth Army, at the north of Brusilov's line, attacked on a 16-mile (26km) front with two corps. After a long artillery bombardment on 4 June, Kaledin unleashed his infantry on the 5th and captured Lutsk by nightfall on the 9th. The Austrian Fourth Army was forced back, and its southern neighbour, the Second Army, also had to withdraw, as the Fourth's retreat exposed its northern flank.

Kaledin's southern neighbour, General Sakharov's Eleventh Army, attacking towards Vorobyevka, was somewhat less successful. The German Southern Army's right, almost all Slav troops, soon folded, but its centre and left held firm.

The guns of the Seventh Army (General Shcherbachev) opened up at 4.00 am on 4 June and continued, with occasional breaks, for 46 hours, shelling wire, trenches and observation posts by day, and firing sporadically during darkness to hinder repairs. At 2.00 am on 6 June, II Corps attacked with two infantry divisions and one regiment on a 4½-mile (7.2km) front; within two hours it took the first two lines of Austrian trenches and most of the third. That evening II Cavalry Corps arrived, and on the 7th the two corps drove the enemy back across the Strypa river. On the 8th the adjacent XVI and XXII Corps joined in on the north, and by the 10th the breach in the Austrian front was 30 miles (48km) wide, with over 16,000 prisoners.

At the front's southern end, Lechitsky's Ninth Army faced Pflanzer-Baltin's Seventh. Lechitsky had only slightly more infantry (10 divisions against eight and a half) and no more cavalry (each had four divisions), but he prepared his attack carefully. He assembled his force in narrow ravines along the Dniestr river that the Austrian artillery could not penetrate, and chose two narrow sectors for the main assault, about 3,000 and 4,000 yds (2,745m and 3,660m) respectively. All 16 battalions of the 3rd Trans-Amur Division assembled in the

Russian infantry charge. Five already casualties. (Ann Ronan Picture Library)

shorter northern sector, and 20, from the
11th and 32nd Divisions, in the southern. His
bombardment began at 4.30 am on 4 June,
and lasted until noon in the southern sector,
12.30 in the northern. As the barrage lifted,
the infantry rushed the Austrian trenches, and
took them all by evening.

Pflanzer-Baltin, under cover of
counter-attacks, prepared to evacuate his east-
bank bridgeheads, and on 10 June pulled back
to the river Prut. Several days of torrential rain
hampered pursuit, so the Austrians averted
total disaster; but they were forced back across
the Prut, retaining only one bridgehead on its
east bank, just north of Czernowitz (now
Chernivtsi), capital of Austrian Bukovina.
Here they held for five days, but on the 19th
XII Corps took Czernowitz, and two days later
Pflanzer-Baltin withdrew to the Seret river.

Thus in the first two weeks Brusilov's two
flank armies, the Eighth and Ninth, achieved
considerable penetrations, but success in the
centre was more limited. Casualties in all
three armies were heavy, and most of the
artillery ammunition had been fired. The
inner flanks of the Eighth and Ninth Armies
were vulnerable to counter-attacks, so the
line needed to be straightened by advancing
the centre. This raised the issue of
pinning-down attacks and the West Front's
passivity. Successful though Brusilov's
offensive was proving, it was officially only a
curtain-raiser for Evert's. That was due to
start on 14 June, but Evert requested four
days' postponement for bad weather, then
claimed that the German concentration of
troops and guns at Molodechno was too
strong to beat, and proposed attacking at
Baranovichi instead. The Tsar consented, but
the need to regroup imposed further delay.

Brusilov protested hotly at being left
unsupported, scorned Evert's Baranovichi
plan as needing at least six weeks to prepare,
and asked Alexeyev to persuade the Tsar to
order Evert to attack as planned. Alexeyev
replied that Evert had orders to attack by
3 July, and offered Brusilov two additional
corps. Brusilov grumbled that Evert's attack
would fail because it could not be properly
prepared so quickly, that two corps were no

compensation for Evert's foot-dragging and
that moving them would take a long time,
during which they would obstruct transport
of his supplies; but he did not refuse them.

Events justified Brusilov's scepticism, and
his fears of German counter-action. When
Evert finally moved, at Lake Narozh and
Baranovichi, he did not even succeed in
pinning any German forces down. The
Germans realised that Brusilov's successes
threatened a death-blow to Austria-Hungary,
and began moving troops south even before
Evert's offensive petered out, on 9 July.

The Somme offensive it was meant to
support was a disaster, and the only bright
spot was the South-West Front. By 23 June it
had taken 204,000 prisoners, so on 24 June
Stavka decided to reinforce success and
temporarily subordinated the Third Army
(General Lesh) to Brusilov. He ordered his
two wings to maintain their offensives, while
the Eleventh Army stood its ground.

The Germans' principal concern was to
hold Kovel because its loss would cut the
north–south railway, hampering movement
between the Austrian and German fronts. A
mixed German–Austrian force was
assembling in the Kovel–Manevichi area to
attack the Eighth Army's north flank, but
Lesh and Kaledin disrupted its preparations
by attacking first, on 4 July.

The Germans then planned a
counter-offensive in the centre, to push back
the Eleventh Army, which had been
weakened by dispatching its reserves to its
neighbours. However, the South-West Front's
spies notified Brusilov that the
counter-offensive was scheduled for 18 July,
and he ordered the Eleventh Army to
pre-empt it. At night on 15 July, Sakharov's
troops attacked north of Brody, taking
13,000 prisoners and, more importantly,
destroying the three dumps of ammunition
stockpiled for the counter-offensive. The
Germans had to call it off.

Elsewhere, however, the Central Powers'
situation looked better. Kaledin was halted
on 8 July, 25 miles (40km) short of Kovel.
His advance to the river Stokhod eliminated
a threat to his right flank, but brought him

no nearer Kovel, now heavily protected by German forces.

Both sides now raced to reinforce. The Germans moved troops from the Western Front, the Austrians from the Italian and Serbian fronts. Stavka sent Brusilov units from the West Front and the rear. Thanks to superior railways, the Central Powers were reinforcing slightly the faster, but not yet fast enough to replace their losses. Brusilov's strengthened north and south flank armies pressed forward, and the Eleventh Army straightened the line in the centre by advancing to the Koshev–Lishnev area, taking another 34,000 prisoners.

The Third and Eighth Armies halted on the Stokhod on 14 July, and began regrouping to advance on Kovel and Vladimir-Volynski. The elite Guard Army now arrived. Commanded by General Bezobrazov, it had four infantry corps (I and II Guard, I and XXX infantry), each of two divisions, and the Guard Cavalry Corps, of three, under General The Khan of Nakhichevan. It was deployed between the Third and Eighth Armies, where its 134,000 men greatly outnumbered the two German and two Austrian divisions facing it.

Brusilov planned to resume his offensive in two stages. The Seventh and Ninth Armies in the south were to start advancing north-west along the Dniestr on 23 July, the Third, the Guard and the Eighth were to follow on 28 July over the Stokhod, the first two towards Kovel, the third towards Vladimir-Volynski, also on the north–south railway. Torrential rain forced postponement in the south, and all attacked on 28 July.

The Stokhod's east bank was marshy and wooded, and the Guards were confined to three narrow causeways. They advanced with all the expected *élan*, driving the mixed Austro-German force across the river and taking some 11,000 prisoners. However, machine guns and marshy terrain exacted an enormous price, as did enemy use of air superiority to deny reconnaissance and impede artillery support by shooting down observation balloons. In its first two weeks at the front (21 July–2 August) the Guard Army

lost about 30,000 men, and Brusilov's belief that Kovel could be taken in a week proved unrealistic. The Eighth Army took 9,000 prisoners, but Vladimir-Volynski also proved beyond reach, and all three northern armies had to dig in against fierce counter-attacks. The Eleventh Army stormed Brody on 28 July, advanced to the Graberka and Seret rivers and took another 8,000 prisoners.

On 3 August Brusilov conferred with Kaledin and Bezobrazov at Lutsk, and decided to continue towards Kovel. The Guard Army's sector was too marshy for cavalry, so its Cavalry Corps was dismounted and used to man quiet sectors, releasing three infantry divisions for the main blow. This would be delivered by I Guards and I Corps north-westward from Velitsk, supported by a westward thrust by I Siberian and XVI Corps of the Third Army north of them, and an assault on the fortified village of Vitoney by the Guard Rifle Division south of them.

It was hoped that concentrating 64 battalions against nine German and 16 Hungarian would overcome the enemy's advantage of prepared positions, and the lack of maps or photographs of the defences – these were mostly in woodland, and German aircraft thwarted attempts to photograph those visible from the air. But the attack, launched on 8 August, failed completely. By next morning the Guard was back on its start line, minus almost 9,000 men. The Third Army fared no better, and the Guard Rifle Division occupied Vitoney, but heavy artillery fire drove it out. Nicholas dismissed Bezobrazov, renamed the Guard the 'Special Army' and removed it. At the same time, mid-August, the Third Army was returned to the West Front, leaving Brusilov only his original four armies.

On 2 August Hindenburg was at last given charge of the entire Eastern Front. However, no sooner had the Austrian General Staff agreed than it partly reneged, stipulating that the two armies south of the Tarnopol–Lemberg railway, the 'German Southern' and the Seventh, should remain under Archduke Charles and Austrian GHQ.

On the southern sector, the Russian Seventh and Ninth Armies pushed together along the river Korobtsa towards the regional centre of Monastryziska, and on 9 August the Ninth Army broke the Austrian line near Stanislav. The Eleventh pushed southwards west of the river Strypa, threatening to outflank Bothmer. The Kaiser had visited Bothmer's positions during the previous winter, and pronounced them impregnable; but now they were untenable. Bothmer withdrew some 10 miles (16km), to the Zlota Lipa river. On 12 August the Ninth Army took Nadworna, and the Seventh Monastryziska. The front in the south then stabilised temporarily.

In the ten weeks to 12 August Brusilov's offensive had captured 8,255 officers and 370,153 men. Including killed and wounded, it had deprived the Central Powers of over 700,000, and taken over 15,000 square miles (38,000km²) of territory, by far the Entente's biggest success so far. Brusilov's unorthodoxy had been brilliantly vindicated.

But the price had been high. Russian casualties were over 550,000, and three-quarters of the Front's 400,000-man reserve had been expended. Success also brought increased commitments in the south, where the Ninth Army's advance into the Carpathian foothills more than doubled its front line. But a much greater additional burden was about to materialise.

# Romanian campaign, September 1916–January 1917

The Entente had long been wooing Romania, which had an interest in joining the war. This interest was Transylvania, Hungarian ruled, but mostly Romanian populated. However, Romania could only hope to get it if the Entente won, and up to mid-1916 that did not look very likely. Besides, should a Central Powers' victory put Transylvania out of reach, Russian Bessarabia (now Moldova), also mostly Romanian populated, could be a consolation prize.

Strategic vulnerability also dictated caution. Romania had very long frontiers relative to its area. Bulgaria had joined the Central Powers in September 1915, had a territorial claim against Romanian Dobrudja and could well pursue it militarily if Romania joined the Entente. Bucharest would then be particularly endangered, as it was only 30 miles (48km) from the Bulgarian border. The Romanian army numbered 23 divisions, but all were poorly equipped and trained, and deficient in wheeled transport; the road system was inadequate, the railways not much better. Prudence probably dictated staying neutral, but Brusilov's successes created a chance for Romania to seize Transylvania while Austria-Hungary was fully stretched, so on 27 August Romania declared war.

One division was left to guard Dobrudja, and almost all the rest were sent into Transylvania. Hungary had few troops there, a few days would suffice to take it, and then Dobrudja could be reinforced. However, as insurance, the Romanian High Command asked Russia for troops, and Alexeyev agreed to send to Dobrudja the minimum three divisions specified by the Russo-Romanian military convention.

Unfortunately, this proved only the first, and smallest, burden that Romania's entry into the war imposed on Russia. Bulgaria was not at war with Russia, and diplomatic manoeuvre and a token military presence might deter it from invading Dobrudja. But Austria-Hungary and Germany were already at war, so diplomacy could not neutralise the threat from Galicia.

To counter it, Alexeyev dispatched seven infantry and one cavalry divisions to the Ninth Army between 23 July and 31 August, one from the rear, the rest by taking one each from the First, Fourth, Fifth and Sixth Armies, two from the Seventh and the cavalry division from the Third. Thus Lechitsky had 17 infantry and five cavalry divisions, although 14 of them, having been in action since 4 June, were understrength.

The Central Powers had grasped the danger that Lechitsky's advance posed, and

Romanian infantry in their trenches, November 1915.
(Ann Ronan Picture Library)

reinforced the Austrian Seventh Army with five German divisions, plus two divisions and two mountain brigades from Austria's Italian front. The Austrian Seventh grew to 16½ infantry and four cavalry divisions. Half its infantry and all its cavalry were in no better shape than Lechitsky's, but the five German divisions were formidable, and so were the Austrian mountain brigades. They had fought in the Dolomites, whereas most Russian soldiers had never seen mountains before, let alone fought in them.

For Dobrudja, Alexeyev could spare only two Russian divisions, while the convention stipulated at least three. A '1st Serbian Volunteer Division' was being formed from prisoners of war, and Alexeyev decided to include it in the 'Dobrudja Detachment'. He was presumably unaware that to find Russia allied with Romanians and Serbs, whom they had fought as recently as 1913, would

extend Bulgarian hostility from them to their Russian mentors.

The South-West Front was partially reorganised. The Special (ex-Guard) Army, now commanded by Gurko, returned, and took over the Eighth Army's northern sector. Reconnaissance reported the enemy positions in the Lutsk salient east of Kovel (held by Linsigen's German 'Army of Manoeuvre' and Archduke Josef Ferdinand's Austrian Fourth) too strong to take, so Brusilov decided to substitute a westward thrust towards Vladimir-Volynski by the Special Army and the right wing of the Eighth. His two centre armies, the Eleventh and Seventh, in line from Brody to Stanislav, were given no major task, as both were much understrength. Two divisions and a corps staff of the Seventh were transferred to its southern neighbour, the Ninth, which received the major assignment for September, and the lion's share of reinforcements. To help secure Romania, it was to seize the north–south passes through the Carpathians.

While Romania was invading Transylvania, and the Russo-Serbian force was moving into Dobrudja, the Ninth Army advanced into the Carpathian foothills on a front of about 75 miles (120km) between Nadworna and Dorna Watra (now Vatra Dorne). Lechitsky had superiority of about two to one in infantry and five to one in cavalry, but his advance was necessarily channelled along three main roads, from Delatyn, Kuty and Cimpulung, which converged at Marmarössziget. His cavalry was almost useless in the hills, and enemy howitzers, deployed on reverse slopes out of sight of his artillery spotters, poured fire down on his troops. For lack of aircraft the Russians could seldom locate them, and could not deal effectively with those they did locate because they had few howitzers and little howitzer ammunition. Morale was high, but shortages, enemy artillery and unfamiliarity with mountain warfare made the going hard.

The Romanians had completely occupied Transylvania by 6 September, but the Central Powers riposted quickly. Falkenhayn's failure at Verdun had led on 28 August to his replacement by Hindenburg and he was appointed to command the German Ninth Army, assembling in Galicia. Bulgaria declared war on Romania on 1 September, and a mixed force under Mackensen immediately invaded Dobrudja, sweeping the Romanian division aside, reducing the 1st Serbian and 61st Russian divisions to 3,000 men each, and forcing them out. On 19 September Falkenhayn entered Transylvania and was as little hindered as Mackensen. On 3 October both won major victories, Mackensen forcing withdrawal north of the Danube, and Falkenhayn retreat

from Transylvania by his win at Kronstadt.

For ten days Falkenhayn rolled the Romanians back towards Lechitsky's troops. Near Dorna Watra, on the night of 13 October, six Romanian battalions decamped. Lechitsky plugged the gap

Romanian dead after the Battle of Kronstadt. (Ann Ronan Picture Library)

temporarily with two cavalry divisions, but the Ninth Army had to take over the empty sector or its flank would be turned.

The South-West Front's mission was no longer to eliminate Austro-Hungary, but to prevent Romania's collapse. This necessitated abandoning Brusilov's offensive, and Nicholas ordered its end on 10 October. The extension of the Ninth Army's front meant an additional army was needed. The Eighth Army's Staff was transferred in mid-October from Lutsk to Czernowitz, the Ninth's front was divided in

Germans man-handling their field weaponry.
(Ann Ronan Picture Library)

two, and most of its troops were allocated
to the new Eighth Army. The Dobrudja
Detachment grew to ten divisions and became
the 'Danube Army', under Sakharov, who was
replaced at the Eleventh by General
Klembovsky.

Eighth Army forces remaining on the
Vladimir-Volynski axis were subordinated to
the Special Army, inflating Gurko's
command to 25 infantry and five cavalry
divisions. It fell to him to throw the last
dice, when on 16–17 October he committed
15 divisions to a final thrust at
Vladimir-Volynski. The German artillery
drove out his infantry wherever they
penetrated German lines, and punished
them further as they withdrew to their own.
After two days of this Gurko called a halt,
and the front settled into the mud and mists
of autumn. Since 4 June the South-West

Front had incurred 1.2 million casualties,
including 212,000 taken prisoner.

The onset of winter brought little relief.
Defence of the Romanian front became
Stavka's main preoccupation because failure
could open the way into Ukraine and the
Russian rear. All offensive plans were scrapped.
The North and West Fronts would undertake
only minor operations, and many of their
units would be sent to the new Romanian
Front, formed from the Danube Army and the
remnants of four Romanian armies. This was
nominally commanded by the Romanian King
Ferdinand, but really by General Sakharov.
Bucharest fell on 6 December. Romanian and
Russian pleas to the French to activate the
expeditionary force at Salonika against
Bulgaria produced no significant result. The
Western Allies pronounced Romania solely
Russia's responsibility; and extension of the
front line by about 250 miles (400km) to the
Black Sea coast forced Russia to provide
55 infantry and 15 cavalry divisions to man it.

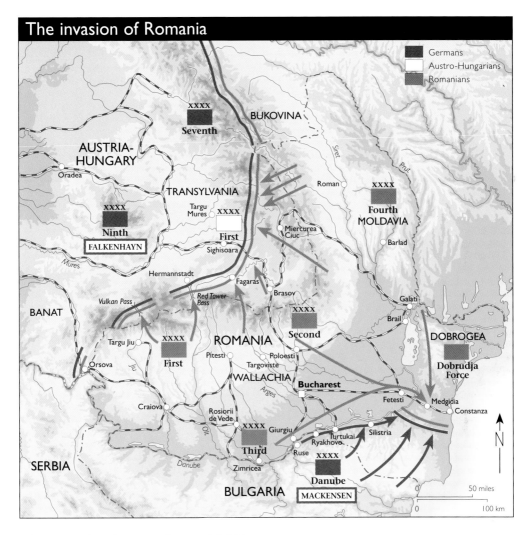

**The invasion of Romania**

Germans
Austro-Hungarians
Romanians

XXXX
Seventh

BUKOVINA

AUSTRIA-HUNGARY

Oradea

TRANSYLVANIA

Roman

XXXX
Fourth
MOLDAVIA

XXXX
Ninth
FALKENHAYN

Targu
Mures

XXXX
First

Miercurea
Ciuc

Sighisoara

Barlad

Mures

Hermannstadt

Fagaras

Brasov

Galati

Vulkan Pass

Red Tower
Pass

XXXX
Second

Brail

BANAT

Targu Jiu

XXXX
First

ROMANIA

DOBROGEA

Orsova

Pitesti

Targoviste

Poloesti

Dobrudja
Force

Craiova

WALLACHIA

Bucharest

Fetesti

Medgidia
Constanza

Rosiorii
de Vede

XXXX
Third

Giurgiu

Turtukai
Ryakhovo

Silistria

SERBIA

Danube

Zimricea

Ruse

XXXX
Danube
MACKENSEN

N

BULGARIA

0          50 miles

0          100 km

## The Russian home front, 1917

Though Ludendorff later admitted that the German army 'had been fought to a standstill, and was utterly worn out', the Germans considered that they had done well enough in the east to transfer eight divisions to the west. They were somewhat surprised when in January–February 1917 the Russian Eighth, Seventh and Ninth Armies attacked, gaining some ground in Bukovina, but at the end of February joint German–Austrian counter-attacks recovered it all.

Meanwhile popular discontent with Nicholas' leadership was increasing and the home front was starting to collapse under the weight of food and fuel shortages, high

prices and continued military failure. On 12 January 1917, British ambassador Buchanan told the Tsar that he must regain the people's confidence. Nicholas' response was: 'Do you mean I am to regain the confidence of my people, or they are to regain my confidence?' Buchanan diplomatically replied 'both', but warned that 'in the event of revolution, only a small part of the army can be counted on to defend the dynasty'. Eight days later Rodzyanko, President of the Duma, delivered a similar warning. But Nicholas took no notice.

February 1917 was a month of extreme cold and heavy snow. The railways were brought almost to a standstill, and

Food riot in Petrograd, March 1917.

Petrograd began to run out of flour, coal and firewood. On 8 March food riots erupted, on the next day crowds began looting bakeries and the Cossacks sent to disperse them fraternised instead, and on the 10th the workers went on strike. On the 11th,

Garrison Commander General Khabalov, on
Nicholas' orders, forbade all public assembly,
but a company of the Pavlovsky Life Guard
Regiment, ordered to fire on a crowd, shot its

officer instead. One after another regimental
commanders notified Khabalov that only
some of their troops were still obeying
orders; and they could not undertake street

duties because if they left barracks the rest would mutiny. By evening on the 12th almost the whole 170,000-man garrison had mutinied, and Khabalov controlled only the Winter Palace, with a mere 1,500 troops.

Revolutionary propagandists had long been at work among the troops, but they did not cause the rising, and no faction stood ready to take over. The Duma hastily set up a 'Provisional Committee' only when it heard on 12 March that a crowd of 80,000 was approaching. By that time an alternative source of power, the Petrograd Soviet, had come into existence.

In 1905 a short-lived 'Soviet (Council) of Workers' Deputies' had been formed to direct a general strike. Now a similar Soviet was set up, mostly by show of hands at open-air meetings. On 13 March both it and the Provisional Committee were at work in the Duma building. That evening Nicholas' ministers resigned, and arrived at the Duma asking to be taken into protective custody.

Nicholas had left on 7 March for Stavka at Mogilev, 500 miles (800km) away. During the next few days Rodzyanko and others advised him that only his abdication could save the monarchy. He attempted to return to Petrograd on 13 March. At 2.00 am on the 14th, when his train arrived at Malaya Vishera, 100 miles (160km) from the capital, he was told that the line to Petrograd was blocked by troops with artillery and machine guns, but he could go east to Moscow or west to Pskov. The North Front's headquarters were at Pskov, so he went

LEFT Soviet myth making. The Winter Palace was not stormed – the Red Guards got in through an unguarded side entrance. (Ann Ronan Picture Library)

ABOVE The Petrograd Soviet in session. (Novosti, London)

The seizure of the Russian Parliament in Petrograd by revolutionary soldiers, 1917. (Ann Ronan Picture Library)

there, to be met by the Front commander, General Ruzhsky, with the news that the entire Petrograd Garrison had mutinied, and four regiments sent to restore order had been stopped on the outskirts, then had deserted *en masse*.

While Nicholas was travelling to Pskov, Rodzyanko spoke to Alexeyev, who agreed that Nicholas must abdicate, and sent telegrams seeking all the Front commanders' opinions. Their replies, received on 15 March, all recommended abdication. That day Nicholas abdicated.

Russia now had no head of state, but it still had a war. A Provisional Government was hastily formed, but the Soviet at once claimed authority over the garrison. On 14 March it issued 'Army Order Number One', proclaiming itself the 'Soviet of Workers' and Soldiers' Deputies' and decreeing that in all political actions military

units must obey only its orders. Discipline must be observed on duty, but off-duty standing to attention and saluting were abolished and titles were replaced by 'Mr General', 'Mr Colonel', etc. Company Committees must control all weapons, and in no circumstances issue any to officers.

The preamble made it clear that the order applied only to the Petrograd Garrison, but copies reached the front, and discipline crumbled in their wake. In April two Duma members visited the front and concluded that the morale of the artillery and Cossacks appeared intact, but the cavalry's was unknown, and much of the infantry 'shaken'.

The German Great General Staff now decided to stir the pot by providing the so-called 'Sealed Train' (actually a carriage) to convey Lenin across Germany to Sweden, whence he arrived in Petrograd on 16 April. There he advocated fraternisation, immediate peace and conversion of the war into a class struggle – that is, civil wars between the peoples and their governments.

Guchkov and his successor, Kerensky, dismissed large numbers of them.

Before the insurrection, Russia had undertaken to co-ordinate its operations with those of Britain and France, and in particular to attack within three weeks of the start of the Anglo-French offensive. Alexeyev, now Commander-in-Chief, notified the Allies that Russia could not meet this commitment until May, and by 12 March he was convinced it could not do so before the end of July. In any case, the army's condition made it impossible to co-ordinate action with Nivelle's offensive in France, scheduled for mid-April.

News of the USA's entry into the war on 6 April offered some encouragement, but was

This was an open challenge to the Provisional Government, whose members saw an Entente victory as essential, since a victorious Germany would restore autocracy. They strove to keep the Eastern Front in being, and prevent enemy transfers to the west, by mounting a summer offensive.

Tension between the Provisional Government and troops increased as Bolshevik and Left Socialist Revolutionary (SR) peace propaganda spread alongside rumours of the impending offensive. However, senior officers remained optimistic, and the West Front told Stavka in mid-April that an offensive would be possible in one or two months, after revolutionary excitement had abated. The Fronts' reports probably erred on the optimistic side because pessimistic officers were deemed counter-revolutionary; War Minister

## The Sealed Train

— Lenin's route from
Zurich to Petrograd

0            500 miles

0            1000 km

SWEDEN

Gulf of Bothnia

Tornio

RUSSIA

FINLAND

Beloostrov

Stockholm

Petrograd

Malmö    Trelleborg

Sassnitz

Berlin            RUSSIA

GERMANY

Berne    Zurich

SWITZERLAND

BELOW Kerensky, War Minister then Prime Minister in
the Provisional Government. He proved no match for
Lenin. (Ann Ronan Picture Library)

followed only ten days later by the collapse
of Nivelle's offensive, and mutinies in the
French army. There was now doubt whether
the Western Front could last out the several
months that would elapse before the
Americans arrived in force, and this
increased Allied anxiety to keep the Eastern
Front in being. They stepped up deliveries,
and soon the material situation was better
than ever.

But psychologically things could hardly
be worse. Guchkov resigned on 1 May, and
on the next day Alexeyev and the Front
commanders addressed a joint meeting of
Provisional Government and Soviet.
Alexeyev told them bluntly that 'the army is
on the brink of ruin', and others gave
instances of the troops' interpretation of
Bolshevik calls for 'peace without
annexations' as meaning they need not
attack even to recover occupied Russian
territory. The Soviet would not act to restore
discipline; the Provisional Government could

Soviet faking. Stalin behind Lenin getting off the train on arrival at Petrograd. Stalin was neither on the train nor at the station. (AKG, Berlin)

not. All that resulted was that on 22 May the new War Minister, Kerensky, replaced Alexeyev with Brusilov, who began planning a scaled-down version of his 1916 offensive, an attempt by the Seventh and Eleventh Armies to take Lemberg, with pinning-down attacks by other Fronts and the Eighth Army (General Kornilov).

# Central Powers advance, July–December 1917

The front had been static since October 1916, the Germans preferring not to risk restoring Russian unity by attacking, so artillery and ammunition were plentiful. A new factor was volunteer shock battalions, which Alexeyev, doubting the ordinary soldier's reliability, had formed from men who specifically asked to continue fighting.

On 18 June the South-West Front's assault began. The shock battalions led the way, but the infantry followed only reluctantly, and after two days refused to go on. On their left, Kornilov attacked on 23 June, against low-quality Austro-Hungarian forces, and took 7,000 prisoners; but as his shock battalions became casualties, the Eighth Army's infantry proved as recalcitrant as the Seventh and Eleventh's. By 2 July the offensive was over. Total losses, 38,700 officers and men, were infinitesimal compared with those tolerated in previous years, but were now unendurable. The Germans and Austrians counter-attacked the Eleventh Army on 6 July, and with nine divisions routed 20, driving the Russians back to the Seret. So complete was the Eleventh's collapse that even its Soldiers' Committees approved shooting of deserters, but apparently no one was prepared to do any shooting.

The North Front's offensive began on 8 July and ended on the 10th. Of six divisions allocated, only two took part, and one of them had to be forced into the line at gunpoint. The other took two lines of German trenches, but then refused to continue and returned to its own lines. When the West Front attempted to attack, with 138 battalions against 17 German, the same happened.

On the Romanian Front the position was slightly better. The Romanian army had greatly improved, and was unaffected by the Russian revolution, so it was planned to use Romanian forces alongside Russian. Here the shock battalions were not used to lead, but deployed behind the troops, to shoot any who ran away. The assault began on 10 July,

and was attended with some success. However, the failures elsewhere had eroded Kerensky's confidence in Brusilov, and he replaced him with the Cossack Kornilov. His first act was to stop the offensive, and the Romanian Front did so on 13 July. From then on, only the Germans would attack.

Nor did the Russians have long to wait. The next German move was near the Baltic coast, where the front, almost unchanged since December 1915, ran along the lower

Germans crossing the Dvina river during the Riga operation, September 1917. No apparent opposition. (Ann Ronan Picture Library)

course of the river Dvina, except for a large Russian bridgehead from 12 miles (19km) above Riga to a point on the coast 25 miles (40km) west of the city. It was held by the Russian Twelfth Army (General Klembovsky), with two corps (II and VI Siberian) in the bridgehead, and another two (XXI and XLIII) behind the Dvina. By August 1917 it was in an advanced state of disintegration. Many soldiers had deserted; those who had not were mostly beyond control by their officers, and had killed many of them. The German Eighth Army (General von Hutier) facing the bridgehead had seven and a half divisions, but was reinforced by eight infantry and two cavalry divisions, and by as much heavy artillery as could be brought up in time from elsewhere on the front.

General Kornilov. (Ann Ronan Picture Library)

Hutier had two options, a frontal assault on the bridgehead, or crossing the Dvina upstream of it and attacking it from behind. The first would involve crossing the estuarine Tirul marshes, the second an opposed river crossing, then taking several fortified positions in succession. He chose the second option, the starting date of 1 September and the place a point about half-way between Jakobshtadt (Jekabpils) and Riga, near two islands, Borkowitz and Elster. After crossing, the main force of three infantry and both cavalry divisions was to head north to the coast, to cut the Twelfth Army's line of retreat towards Petrograd. A second force of two divisions was to follow, to reinforce the main body and guard its flank against any counter-attack from the landward side.

The Russians knew of Hutier's preparations, but misread them as presaging an assault on the bridgehead. So Klembovsky removed his least reliable divisions from there to the east bank of the Dvina, and, fortuitously, deployed them precisely where Hutier intended to cross.

From 4.00 am on 1 September the Germans fired gas shells for two hours, then changed to high explosive. The two islands were taken by 9.00 am, and ten minutes later the river crossing began. The Russian positions were mostly found abandoned; by 5.00 pm the bridgehead was $7^1/_2$ miles (12km) wide, and two lines had been taken. But for once the Russians moved faster than the Germans. Hutier learned early on 2 September that Klembovsky had evacuated the bridgehead, and with his few reliable units as rearguard, was retreating along the Riga–Pskov road and railway, which the Germans had not yet reached. By the time they did, on the afternoon of the 4th, most of the Twelfth Army had gone. The Germans gained much territory and took 24,000

The Kaiser in Riga, September 1917. (Ann Ronan Picture Library)

prisoners, but failed to destroy the Twelfth Army. That proved not to matter; apart from brief German actions to seize three islands at the mouth of the Gulf of Riga (12–20 October), the front remained quiescent until on 7 November the Bolsheviks seized power and began taking Russia out of the war.

The fiasco of the 1917 offensive had shown the depths to which the army's morale had sunk, and on 12 July the Provisional Government had voted to restore both capital punishment and courts-martial. Kerensky was now Prime Minister, but the government was still competing with the Soviet for the loyalty of the armed forces, and had just survived a premature attempt to seize power by a Bolshevik faction. He could not therefore implement the draconian

Krylenko, appointed Commander-in-Chief after the Bolsheviks seized power. He at once asked the Germans for an armistice. (Novosti, London)

measures that Kornilov wanted, so Kornilov began plotting to take power himself. The Cossacks looked to him for leadership, and he had in particular the support of the Don Cossack Ataman (Headman), General Kaledin. The Allies backed Kornilov, seeing his efforts to restore discipline as the only guarantee of Russia's staying in the war, while conservative Russian politicians and financiers backed him as defender against a Bolshevik takeover.

He concentrated III Cavalry Corps (mostly Cossacks) near Petrograd, and arranged to have about 2,000 'Kornilovist' officers posted to the capital. The putsch was to begin by provoking riots, then marching troops into the city on the pretext of protecting the government, while the 2,000 officers would arrest the leaders of all left-wing parties and seize the government buildings. It was planned to take place not later than 1 September.

Kornilov's intentions became known, so Kerensky ordered Kornilov to Petrograd, and when he began to move troops proclaimed him a traitor. But Kerensky had no real force at his disposal, and it was the Soviet that stopped Kornilov. It armed the workers (including Bolshevik Red Guards, who thus obtained thousands of weapons to use later), ordered railway workers to block movement of troops by train, and fetched in sailors from the Baltic Fleet's Kronstadt base. Representatives who went to meet Kornilov's troops persuaded them on 27 August to refuse to go further. The Soviet also told the front-line troops what was happening; many Kornilovist senior officers, including the South-West Front's commander, Denikin, and all his army commanders, were arrested by their men. The Soviet gained most from Kornilov's attempt to establish a military dictatorship, and its failure showed that the army and population had lost interest in the war. The German capture of Riga a few days later passed almost unnoticed.

Kornilov's failure further fragmented the army. The men now saw their officers as the chief obstacles to peace, and many moderate military committees were replaced by radical ones. Bolshevik and German propaganda exploited war-weariness to increasing effect, and by the time the Bolsheviks seized power on 7 November (25 October by the old calendar), the armys' attitude, as described in Stavka's report for the second half of October, was 'one of highly nervous expectancy. Now, as before, irresistible thirst for peace, universal desire to leave the front ... constitute the main motives on which the attitude of most of our troops is based. The army is simply a huge, weary, shabby and ill-fed mob of angry men, united by their common thirst for peace and common disappointment.'

On 25 November the newly appointed Communist Commander-in-Chief, Krylenko, sent a peace delegation to the German lines. General Hoffman replied on the 27th, indicating willingness to grant an armistice. It took effect on 17 December, and both sides prepared to negotiate peace.

# A trooper, an ensign and a sergeant

German Eastern Front soldiers were regularly required to beat numerically superior Russian forces, and almost invariably did. Their leaders seldom exposed them to pointless risk, and normally fed, equipped and rested them adequately. The infantryman could see that his artillery, machine-gun and air support was vastly superior to the Russian, and his feeling of having the edge seldom left him. There was no breakdown of morale in 1918 comparable to that on the Western Front; it was historical irony that, after the failure of a strategy explicitly devised to avoid a two-front war, Germany fought one for three and a half years successfully enough to eliminate one of the fronts, then conceded defeat on the single front in only eight more months.

The heterogeneous Austro-Hungarian forces were not much better equipped than the Russians, and about 60 per cent of them were Slavs – Czechs, Slovaks, Poles, Slovenes, Croats, Bosnian Serbs and Ruthenians. Most of these initially fought reliably, but in time became less reliable, especially the Czechs, who were encouraged to surrender or defect by a reconnaissance unit of Czechs living in the Russian Empire. Attempts to form units from them were initially frustrated by the Tsar's reluctance to arm them while his own troops lacked weapons, then by the Czechs' unwillingness to fight for a Russia that refused public support for Czech independence (the Tsar feared 'infection' spreading to his non-Russian subjects), and by other ministries' desire to use them as industrial or agricultural labour. Some units were formed, but too late to affect the Eastern Front war, though one, the Czechoslovak Legion, played a prominent part in the ensuing Civil War.

The Russian view of military service was expressed in a four-line verse: 'clever to the artillery, drinker to the navy, rich to the cavalry, stupid to the infantry'. It was meant for newly commissioned officers, but the 20–25 per cent of literate conscripts tended to be sent to the artillery or cavalry, and the rest to the infantry. The average soldier could keep no diary or journal, and in the turmoil that followed the 1917 collapse, almost nothing was published about the ordinary soldier's experiences. However, enough military censorship reports survived to give a general picture, and significant accounts were written later by a cavalry Trooper and Sergeant, and an infantry junior officer (Ensign).

The three soldiers served on the same front (South-West), in different units; their accounts are generally consistent with each other, and with the censors' reports. All three were villagers, the Trooper and Sergeant born into peasant families, the Ensign son of a village priest. They were typical in that their families subsisted only by their fathers taking on extra work, and their mothers and sisters making gloves and mittens for sale during winter. They were untypical in receiving education – the Ensign (intended for the priesthood) to the age of 19, the others to the age of ten – and in 'escaping' their rural background early, the Ensign to a theological seminary, the others apprenticed to a shoemaker and a furrier. The Trooper was conscripted in 1912, the others in 1915 – the Ensign in January, the Sergeant in August.

The Ensign underwent officer training from February to May 1915. The programme paid much attention to drill, but taught nothing about surviving on battlefields dominated by 'field obstacles' (trenches, barbed wire, machine guns), or about the possible roles of motor vehicles and aircraft, and next to nothing about co-operation between the different arms of service. He joined an infantry regiment as an Ensign in autumn 1915, and noted that the Russian trenches were primitive, uncomfortable and badly laid out compared to those of the opposing Austrian Seventh Army (the Trooper made the same point after inspecting abandoned Russian and German trenches in 1916). The soldiers had no blankets; and slept in their greatcoats.

The regiment was entirely equipped with captured Austrian rifles, and had only two machine guns per battalion; the artillery was short of howitzers, heavy guns and ammunition of all calibres. After rest and training during the winter, the regiment returned to the line for Brusilov's offensive. The men, and most of the officers, welcomed facing Austrians, not Germans, and heaved collective sighs of relief when shell-bursts showed the pink smoke of Austrian high-explosive, an indication of the moral ascendancy that the Germans had established over the Russian soldier by mid-1916.

The Trooper was at war from the outset. Like the Sergeant he noted the lack of contact between officers and men, and that soldiers were frequently beaten for minor infractions. The Ensign was told to impose discipline by the 'Prussian rule', that 'the soldier must fear the Corporal's stick more than the enemy's bullet'. The Sergeant noted 'One aim was pursued, the soldier was to be an obedient automaton ... The regulations did not provide for corporal punishment, but it was rather widely employed.'

Career officers came from the richer families, and few attempted to adapt to wartime circumstances, in which officer casualties could only be replaced by commissioning the less privileged, such as the Ensign, or promoting warrant officers and sergeants. For example, two sergeants in the Trooper's regiment, decorated for bravery and promoted to Ensign, 'were suddenly posted to another regiment; our regiment's officers and gentlemen were unwilling to shake hands with ex-rankers'. He went on to say:

when the general withdrawal [from Galicia in 1915] began ... depression became more and more marked, and derogatory comments about the High Command became frequent ...

*Reinforcements reaching us from the rear depressed us even more with their talk of imminent famine and our rulers' incompetence. The troops also found it hard to tolerate our officers' disregard for their most basic needs.*

The Sergeant said that during training he saw his Company Commander only twice, and that both times the officer was drunk. He described lack of rapport and unity

The Czech Legion. It took control of the Trans-Siberian Railway, by armoured train and improvisation. (AKG Berlin)

between officers and men as the most characteristic feature of the Tsarist army, though, contradictorily, he also gave instances of considerate and understanding officer behaviour. He also noted that the influx of officers from less privileged backgrounds improved relations up to battalion level, but that the higher commands remained dominated by officers 'alien' to the soldiers.

The typical Russian soldier with whom these three men served was a peasant who, unlike them, had not 'escaped' his background. He lived in a village with no electricity, gas, piped water or sewers, served by unsurfaced roads that were impassable for several weeks at a time during the autumn rains and spring thaw. He was used to hardship and a monotonous diet, described in another popular epigram as 'cabbage soup and buckwheat porridge', and to ill-treatment by 'gentry', whether landlords, factory owners, or his military superiors. He was also, however, unused to handling and maintaining even the simplest machinery. Only the literate minority could do the paperwork of administration, and if they became battle casualties, a unit could soon find itself short of food, fodder or ammunition, or unable to operate the primitive radios used for communicating with higher formations.

Another junior officer, serving on the West Front in February 1916, summed up his men optimistically in a letter home:

*Whomever you ask 'well, brother, fed up with sitting around?' replies, '… we'd like to go forward now. We've got shells, we can push on …'. And in our brigade they've all been under fire, they're experienced soldiers … they survived the painful time when we had no shells … people*

A priest visits a primitive military hospital. (Ann Ronan Picture Library)

*here don't weep or grieve, they're just full of energy and faith in the future, they can even joke happily in their own circle, here you don't meet mournful, sad faces, calm and confidence are written on them … about the war, in the sense of assessing results, betrayals or horrors, they don't talk; rest is devoted to laughter and gossip.*

His assessment was made before the allies' unsuccessful offensives on the Russian West Front of March and July 1916, and his subsequent letters made no reference to his men's morale. The Trooper, Sergeant and Ensign, and the military censors' reports, point to its deterioration during 1916, particularly in its last few months. The Sergeant, en route to the front in August 1916, mentioned conversations with wounded, from which he learned that 'our armies were very poorly armed, the senior commanders had a bad reputation, it was widely held among the soldiers that traitors, bought by the Germans, sat in the High Command, and the troops were poorly fed'. He went on to say that in September 1916 disaffection among the troops mounted, 'especially after letters from home told them of hunger and dreadful disorganisation'. In October he was seriously

wounded, and he returned to the front only in December, where 'talking with the men I realised they were not burning with a desire to "sniff gunpowder", and didn't want the war. They already had different thoughts, about land and peace.'

Estimates of Russia's losses differ considerably, but on the latest available assessment 1.45 million were killed, 3.41 million captured, 3.22 million wounded and over 1 million missing. The ratio of 251 captured or missing to every 100 dead was far the highest for any of the belligerents. In the first two years, the captures resulted mostly from inept generalship, but in 1916–17 they were accompanied by high rates of desertion, indicating erosion of the will to fight. The signs of decay began to accumulate in the last months of 1916.

Russia contributed troops to the Anglo-French forces in Greece. They went by ship to a French Channel port, then by train to Marseilles. On 2 August 1916 soldiers travelling by train from Marseilles to embark for the Salonica front, beat their commanding officer to death. Their comrades refused to identify the killers until threatened with the shooting of every tenth man. Twenty-six were court-martialled, and eight of them shot. The men were officially said to have been exposed to revolutionary propaganda while in transit camp in Marseilles, but there had already been disorders aboard ship between Archangel and France.

Unrest was not exceptional, as military censors' reports showed, and the commanders knew it was fragile. However, optimists, such as Brusilov's General Quartermaster, Dukhonin, expected the winter lull to provide relief, and morale to be much improved by the spring of 1917.

That this view was unrealistic soon became apparent. On 1 and 2 October 1916, in the Eastern Carpathians, two Siberian regiments of the Seventh Army refused orders to attack. On 9 October a regiment of the Special (ex-Guard) Army was forced at gunpoint by the two adjacent regiments to cease working on defences. Another threatened to fire on its neighbours if they obeyed orders to attack. Two more regiments were found to have been distributing peace propaganda for several months, including an anti-war manifesto written by the commanding officer of one of them; this in an 'elite' army raised in 1915, with specially selected officers and men.

In April 1916 the head of the Petrograd Okhrana (Security) could write: 'The Petrograd Garrison does not believe Russian arms can succeed, and finds prolongation of the war useless, but soldiers in fighting units express confidence that victory is possible.' By the end of 1916, this distinction was disappearing. Military censors' reports referred both to the depressive effect of letters from home ('Almost every letter … expresses a wish for the war to end as soon as possible'), and to the disgruntled tone of many soldiers' letters.

Food and fuel shortages and escalating prices affected morale. The Petrograd Military Censorship Commission on 27 November quoted soldiers' complaints of shortages of food, warm clothing and equipment, and added, 'in letters from the army, just as mostly in letters to the army, dissatisfaction begins showing itself more and more acutely about the country's internal political situation … Rumours reach the army about disorders, strikes in factories, and mutinies in rear units, and cause morale to decline.'

To free Russian troops for the front line, the Tsar on 25 June 1916 had ordered conscription for non-combatant duties from populations hitherto exempt, including the Muslims of Turkestan (to provide 250,000), and Steppe (243,000) Governorates. This sparked risings throughout central Asia, which continued until December; barely had they been put down, and about half the desired numbers conscripted, when the regime collapsed.

Even had the full number been available, they would have made little difference. A report to Alexeyev on 15 October 1916 estimated that reserves available after 1 November would total only 1.4 million, almost all of low quality: 350,000 aged

37–40, 700,000 youths not due for conscription until 1919, and 200,000 previously rejected as physically unfit. Even with replacements cut to 300,000 a month, numbers would begin to fall from March 1917. This decline was accelerated, but not caused, by the events of 1917.

In 1914 nationalism had prevailed over class solidarity among most European socialists. A small minority, led by Vladimir Ilich Ulyanov (Lenin), argued for turning the 'imperialist' war into a class war, in which the conscripts, instead of fighting other countries' conscripts, would turn their guns on their rulers. The revolutionaries' linking of anti-war sentiment, social reforms, especially land reform, and opposition to the autocracy had some early effect. In January 1915, the Interior Ministry noted that many soldiers' letters home instructed the recipients to stop paying rent for their land; the Grand Duke ordered them destroyed. The revolutionaries then intensified their propaganda among training units in the rear, worrying the Grand Duke enough for him to have the Orthodox Church Synod ask bishops to appoint as chaplains experienced priests, capable of 'countering corruption by revolutionary propaganda'.

However, the success of anti-war propaganda among troops in the rear was not yet matched in the front line. There the shared purpose of self-preservation, unit pride, comradeship among men who had been under fire together, and measures taken to keep out anti-war propaganda, defeated Bolshevik efforts. The party then infiltrated members into the military zone, but on 26 May 1915, the Grand Duke prohibited front-line visits by persons of 'dubious political reliability', and had some leaflet distributors exiled to Siberia.

Foiled yet again, the Bolsheviks ordered party members without police records to volunteer for military service. This was much harder to counter, as fellow-soldiers would hardly betray an agitator, even if they rejected his views. From then until the regime's collapse, subversives in uniform were a source of anxiety to the military leadership.

The socialist parties organised a conference in September 1915 in Switzerland, aimed at trying to end the war by international working-class action. Most participants supported a vague appeal to workers to 'struggle for peace', but Lenin headed a minority who advocated civil wars of peoples against their rulers there and at a second conference in April 1916. Lenin did not speculate on what would happen if Russians answered the call while Germans did not, because he believed that revolutions were imminent, and would render frontiers and nationalism obsolete.

As the 1916 campaigning season approached, revolutionary propaganda intensified, including spreading false rumours that soldiers on both sides were already refusing orders to attack. Henceforth claims that German troops were mutinous and Germany ripe for revolution became increasingly prominent in Bolshevik propaganda. The front-line soldiers knew they were false, but troops in the rear and civilians were more credulous. On 14 April 1916, the head of the Petrograd Okhrana reported: '[Petrograd Garrison] soldiers say openly that … revolution has already begun in Germany, and as soon as success has been achieved there, we shall follow Germany's example.'

In fact the Germans had other reasons to keep the Eastern Front quiescent. They were withdrawing troops from there for the Verdun offensive, they had also had to help Bulgaria and Austria-Hungary conquer Serbia, and they saw no point in attacking in the winter snow or the spring mud. No offensive could be decisive, given Germany's commitments elsewhere, and to mount one might make the Russians sink their differences.

One reason for the impact of anti-war propaganda was military reliance solely on repression to maintain discipline. Stavka never attempted persuasion, or even telling the troops why Russia was at war – the Trooper said that only by talking to officers' orderlies did the men learn that Russia was

A dead Russian soldier lies where he fell. (AKG Berlin)

about to go to war. To explain the autocrat's decisions implicitly undermined the principle that they must be obeyed unquestioningly; but eschewing counter-indoctrination meant taking the troops' docility for granted, an ever less realistic attitude as time passed.

In the circumstances, it was surprising not that Russian troops sometimes performed badly, but that they often performed well. Defeatist revolutionary activities constantly worried the High Command, but the examples cited above suggest that reliability was the norm, not the exception, among front-line units until the last quarter of 1916. And in March 1917 it was not the front-line troops but the Petrograd Garrison that mutinied and brought down the regime.

Three of the four sources cited above were chosen because of their subsequent careers.

The Sergeant was Georgiy Zhukov, of the 10th Novgorod Dragoons. The Ensign, later Staff-Captain, was Alexander Vasilevsky of the 409th Infantry Regiment, and the Trooper Alexander Gorbatov of the Chernigov Hussars. All three rose high in the Red Army. In the Second World War, Zhukov and Vasilevsky, both Marshals, held its two top posts, respectively Deputy Supreme Commander and Chief of General Staff, and masterminded the victories that eluded their Tsarist predecessors. Gorbatov became a full General and commanded an army. Their views 'from below' can therefore be taken as fairly authoritative. The fourth source, Alexander Zhiglinsky, who assessed his men so optimistically in February 1916, was less fortunate. He was invalided out of the army in December 1916, went to the Crimea and took no part in the Civil War. In December 1920 the newly installed Soviet authorities there shot all ex-Tsarist officers.

# The last days of Tsarist Russia

Throughout the war Russia's main problem was supplying its troops with the necessities of war, and its cities with food and fuel. Russia's size, an asset in some other respects, was a drawback when it came to meeting these objectives. Its thinly spread railway system could cope with peacetime loads, but the war soon overloaded it. First came the transport of reservists to their units, and of units (men, guns, horses, carts) to the front. Then came the burden of maintaining a regular supply to the army of food, ammunition, weapons and (the largest single item) fodder for horses. Added to that was the increase in industrial demand, particularly for coal.

Most of the heavy industry was in the north-west of European Russia, particularly in the Petrograd and Moscow areas, and was fuelled in peacetime, as also were most households, by Welsh coal delivered by ship to the Baltic ports. When Germany closed off access to or from the Baltic, coal had instead to come by rail from mines in Ukraine, over 1,000 miles (1,600km) away, and a crisis in coal supply began a mere six months into the war. Similarly, Turkey's entry into the war closed off access to the Black Sea ports, and the Allies' failure at Gallipoli to reopen the Turkish Straits cut off Russia's possibilities for importing machine tools, weapons and ammunition via the Mediterranean.

External links could be maintained only through Vladivostok in the Far East and Archangel on the north coast. Vladivostok had good port facilities, and icebreakers could keep them working in winter. But it was 6,000 miles (10,000km) from the front line, and necessitated immensely long transits, first across the Pacific and then via the mostly single-track Trans-Siberian Railway. And until July 1916, when a major

bridge over the Amur west of Khabarovsk was completed, everything had to be ferried across the river. Ships delivered supplies faster than the Trans-Siberian could remove them, so they piled up on the wharves.

The sea and rail routes via Archangel were much shorter, but the port froze for almost half the year; a subsidiary port, Ekonomiya, was constructed downriver, and was ice free for most months, but its capacity was limited, and it had not been open long before the regime collapsed. Ships could deliver in six months more than the railway, also single-track, could remove in a year, and here, too, cargoes piled up. The Gulf Stream kept the north-coast fishing village of Alexandrovsk (now Murmansk) ice free, and a railway was being built to it, but it was completed only at the end of 1916, less than three months before the collapse.

Attempts to improve domestic supply began in March 1915, when the Ministry of Transport was empowered to control fuel producers. In May, after the supply crisis spread to food and fodder, the Ministry of Commerce and Industry was given powers to control agricultural supplies, food prices and the supply of food and fodder to the army. But attempts by the ministry and municipalities to control supplies and prices foundered on inefficiency, corruption, lack of funds and the declining capacity of the railways. In 1914 Russia had just over 20,000 locomotives and about 540,000 rail wagons. Those were modest enough totals (Britain, one-hundredth the area of Russia, had more locomotives), but by 1917, through labour and materials shortages and plain bad management, they had shrunk to 9,000 and 150,000 respectively. Inevitably, supplies of fuel and food to the cities suffered, and when the bad weather of February 1917 put 1,200 locomotives out of action with boilers or piping burst by freezing of the water inside them, food and fuel vanished from Petrograd. The food riots that began on 8 March escalated into revolution, and the Tsar abdicated a week later.

Considering that it was originally meant only as a diversion, the Brusilov offensive was a remarkable feat. It brought Austria-Hungary close to collapse, and forced both it and Germany to transfer troops from elsewhere. Forty-three divisions (15 from the Western Front, 19 from elsewhere on the Eastern Front, seven from Italy and two from Turkey) were so transferred. Their removal both weakened the German effort at Verdun and forced Falkenhayn to abandon plans to disrupt the expected Somme offensive by attacking first. The Austrians could not exploit their success against the Italians in the Trentino because they had to transfer seven divisions to the East.

But the need to sustain Romania saw no fewer than 27 Russian divisions sent there in the ten weeks following its declaration of war. The Allied failure on the Somme enabled the Germans to send troops east to bolster their faltering Austro-Hungarian allies, and Falkenhayn's dismissal was another negative consequence for the Entente, as the far more formidable Hindenburg–Ludendorff team replaced him. Even so, the success was remarkable for an army that had suffered so many serious defeats in the previous two years. Brusilov's novel tactic of eschewing concentration and instead 'nibbling' simultaneously at a large number of points, initially proved itself; but the Russian regime and armed forces collapsed before any Russian generals could emulate it. And despite the improvements in supply wrought by General Polivanov, Russian armies remained technically inferior to their opponents, particularly the Germans. Casualties were inevitably high and the biggest casualty of all was the Russian soldiers' morale, which collapsed dramatically in 1917.

Throughout the war Nicholas, urged on by Alexandra and Rasputin, refused to dilute his autocratic powers, which he sincerely believed were God given, by forming a government based on majority support in the Duma. But public discontent was such that some spreading, if not of responsibility for decisions, at least of the odium they incurred, would have been advisable. The summer 1915 Duma session (19 June–3 September) offered an opportunity, when a new group, the 'Progressive Bloc', was formed. It was supported by all except the extreme left- and right-wing parties, comprised over two-thirds of the Duma, and demanded representative government. Nicholas' only response was to prorogue the Duma, and he recalled it only after nation-wide demonstrations.

Alexandra constantly attacked Cabinet ministers who incurred Rasputin's or her displeasure. With the Tsar away at Stavka, his normal receptiveness to her suggestions increased, and from mid-1915 capable ministers were replaced by nonentities. First of these was the replacement of Goremykin as Prime Minister by Stürmer, a notorious pro-German. Next was the War Minister, General Polivanov. In the few months since he replaced the incompetent Sukhomlinov, he had effected immense improvements in army supply and training. However, like Grand Duke Nikolay, he hated Rasputin and favoured seeking Duma support, a combination that doomed him in Alexandra's eyes. On 25 March 1916, Nicholas replaced him with General Shuvayev, whom coming events would show to be a poor substitute.

Foreign Minister Sazonov's liberalism also made him suspect to Alexandra. In particular, she saw his advocacy of a post-war united autonomous Poland, linked to Russia only by acknowledging the Tsar as head of state, as threatening her husband's present and son's future autocratic rule, because other provinces would be likely to demand the same status. Nicholas dismissed him in July 1916, despite British and French protests. Sturmer added Sazonov's duties to his own, to the further detriment of relations with Britain and France, which deemed him totally untrustworthy.

But the most disastrous appointment Alexandra and Rasputin engineered was that

of Alexander Protopopov in October 1916 as Minister of the Interior. To his control of the police Alexandra then added responsibility for food distribution. Given the poor state of the railways, a much more effective minister would have had difficulty maintaining food supplies to the cities in the 1916–17 winter. Protopopov found it impossible, and his fifth and last month in office ended with food riots that escalated into revolution, and brought the regime down within a week. Rasputin had been assassinated on 31 December 1916 by ultra-monarchists who wanted to save the regime by purging it of his malign influence, but it was too late.

The Provisional Government's attempt to keep Russia in the war was only to a very minor extent governed by the undertaking Russia had given in the Treaty of London not to make a separate peace. The main reason for it was that if the Central Powers won the war, autocracy would be restored in the rump Russian state that they would permit to exist. The mutinies in the French army in April 1917 marked the low point of the Entente's fortunes, raising at least to outsiders the question of whether the Western Front could last out until the Americans arrived.

The Allies were painfully aware of the effect an additional 40 or more enemy divisions could have if transferred from the east. But apart from their natural distaste for Lenin's calls on their workers to overthrow them, the Allies' governments cherished two illusions. The first, that the Bolsheviks were German agents, had some basis in fact, and the Germans shared it for a while. They had eased Lenin's return to Russia so that he could erode its will to fight, and he had done just that. They had not, however, expected him to come to power, and he kept calling on German and Austrian workers, peasants and soldiers to follow Russia's example and overthrow their rulers.

The Allied governments' second illusion was not shared by the Germans, and had no

factual basis. It was the belief that there were large numbers in Russia who wanted to continue the war. In that belief the Allies stepped up deliveries of military equipment to unprecedented levels. However, the railways' capacity to move them had declined almost to nothing, and the army for which they were intended was melting away. Huge stocks accumulated at Archangel and Vladivostok, and some at the ice-free port of Alexandrovsk (Murmansk), to which a railway had just been completed. Among the reasons for the Allied intervention in formally non-belligerent Russia was the fear that the Bolshevik government would hand these stocks over to the Germans.

The Brest-Litovsk Treaty was signed on 3 March 1918. British troops landed at Murmansk in May; British, French and American troops at Archangel in July; Japanese, American, British and French at Vladivostok in July and August; and also in August British troops were fighting the Turks at Baku, attempting to prevent a Central Powers takeover of the oilfields. Meanwhile the Germans were in the Baltic provinces and Finland and, together with the Austro-Hungarians, in Ukraine.

These interventions had a mixture of motives. Germany and Austria-Hungary wanted Ukrainian food, coal and iron ore, and Caspian oil. Japan had imperialist designs on part of the Russian Far East. Turkey wanted to recover Kars, Ardahan and Batum, which Russia had annexed in 1878, and add Georgia and Azerbaijan to them. All the European governments on both sides, and the US administration, took the Bolshevik calls for revolutions seriously, perhaps more seriously than the masses to whom they were directed. They saw the new Russian government as dangerous enough to justify crusading against it, the Entente powers having the additional motive of keeping the stockpiled supplies out of German hands.

However, to the Bolsheviks the fact that countries that elsewhere were fighting each other were, as they saw it, all making common cause against Communism,

appeared to justify their view of capitalism as a worldwide conspiracy of the rulers against the peoples. The siege mentality that characterised the Soviet Union for most of its

German troops in Ukraine, 1918. (AKG Berlin)

existence originated in the months following the signing of the Treaty of Brest-Litovsk.

# 'Living on cereals and porridge'

Before the war Germany imported about one-third of its food, including 12 per cent of fats and 28 per cent of proteins, so the civilian population suffered increasing shortages of flour, butter, cooking fat and meat as the war progressed. By mid-1916, weekly meat consumption had fallen from the pre-war 21/2lb to 1lb (1.13kg to 0.45kg), flour from 5lb to 21/2lb (2.27kg to 1.13kg), and fats from 14oz to 4oz (400g to 114g). Not only was the quantity more than halved, but the quality fell; the wartime flour contained much bran, the meat much bone and gristle. The reduced rations were partly a consequence of cessation of imports, especially grain, from Russia, but resulted mainly from the blockade. German civilians were not actually starving, but malnutrition was becoming widespread enough to arouse popular discontent.

The wave of strikes that began in April 1917 owed something to the Petrograd Soviet's call for 'peace without annexations or indemnities', but more to the hardships of the just-ended 'Turnip winter' (so called because turnips often had to substitute for unavailable potatoes), and a cut in the bread ration from 4lb to 3lb (1.81kg to 1.36kg) a week. The Social Democrats and others in the Reichstag could argue about the need for peace, but the military-dominated leadership wanted a victor's peace, and with America just entering the war, there was no way the Entente powers would give it to them. The civilian population simply had to continue suffering, with only such sporadic relief as foodstuffs delivered from conquered Romania under the armistice it signed in December 1917, or that Ukraine undertook to deliver in return for Germany's recognition of its independence in February 1918.

Austria-Hungary's civilian population suffered similar hardships, again mostly caused by the blockade, but exacerbated by difficulties in maintaining food production when most able-bodied peasants were in the army and rail distribution was disrupted by military traffic. As in Germany, there were widespread strikes in Austria-Hungary in early 1917; here, too, they owed more to hunger than to the Russian revolutionary example.

As in all the other belligerents, how the war affected Russia's civilians depended on where they lived and how a family's breadwinners earned their livings. The effects were more acute than elsewhere for several reasons. The standard of living was very low to begin with, and sank more as the war progressed. Agriculture was almost totally dependent on muscle power, and rural families suffered when the army conscripted most of the able-bodied peasants. In the winter it was common for male peasants to seek work in towns, often 100 miles (160km) away or more, and their wages, though small, were more than the allowances paid to their families when they were conscripted – moreover, after mid-1915 the allowance was terminated if the soldier was captured.

The most detailed descriptions of peasant life come from the relatively small number who 'escaped' from it. One fairly typical example was as follows:

The family had ten children. Large families were common because there were no social services, so the parents needed the children's labour and later their support in old age, and some of the children were likely to die in infancy. Clothes were bought new only for the eldest boy and girl, and handed down, increasingly patched, to the younger ones. The family had one cow, which the mother tended, but its milk went to market, and so did its annual calf, because the grain and potatoes they grew were never enough to last the year, and the money was needed to buy bread. There was also a horse, always an old one, bought cheaply, and carefully skinned when it died, as the money obtained for the skin went towards purchase of its replacement. The nearby woods and marshes provided mushrooms and berries, the best sold, the worst eaten, hay and fodder for the cow and horse, and wood for fires. In the winter all males over 12 years of age went to the nearby town and worked cleaning sheepskins. The wages were meagre, but they were allowed to keep the wool scraped off the skins, and this was taken home for their womenfolk to spin and make into mittens for sale. Many girls aged 12 or over worked in textile factories in the nearby town. The author of the account had three years' schooling, from age seven to ten, then went to join his father cleaning sheepskins.

The effects of the war on a family already barely subsisting were serious. The three eldest brothers were called up, and two of them were killed; the money they contributed from their work, and their labour at harvest time, ceased on call-up, and were replaced only by a small allowance paid in respect of one of them. When the surviving son arrived home in March 1918 he found his father ill, the house and outbuildings in a ruinous state, and no seed grain or potatoes left for sowing. Survival was possible only because the men of his regiment, before decamping, had shared out the regimental stores among themselves, and he was able to sell his portion to buy seed.

Most peasants saw the February–March revolution as a signal to drive out the landlords and divide their estates among themselves. Mass desertions from the army took place during the summer and autumn of 1917 when the soldiers, overwhelmingly peasants, headed for home to ensure they got their fair share of redistributed land. A governess on one estate described the consequences:

*the garden very much spoilt by the peasants and miners, who already considered it theirs by right, and we had to stay near our home or run the risk of being insulted … we left with the sad feeling that we looked for the last time upon the*

*dear old place. And so it was, for a few months later it lay in a heap of ruins.*

The war's effects on town dwellers were equally drastic. Food supplies dwindled because only women, children, the old, unfit or disabled were left to grow them. The 1915 harvest was so poor that even in the grain-growing Volga provinces flour-mills were periodically idle, while elsewhere they stopped for months for lack of grain. Even in the bread-basket of Ukraine and North Caucasus, the cities and towns reported flour and bread shortages, while meat and sugar also became scarce. Not one of the main cities abounded in all four; many lacked them all. Some residents had 'dachas' (smallholdings outside town) and planted vegetables there in their free time, but increasingly often they arrived to find the produce had been stolen.

Food prices rose in all the warring countries, but more in Russia than elsewhere. Compared to 1913–14, by early 1916 they were up 50–70 per cent in Britain, and 20–50 per cent in France. But in Russia the increases averaged 114 per cent, and in some cities were much larger. For example, in Moscow in June 1916 butter was 220 per cent, beef 371 per cent, mutton 381 per cent and rye bread 150 per cent above July 1914 levels. Fuel and clothing prices increased comparably, while wages, very low in 1914, had less than doubled. Municipalities' attempts to cap price increases merely drove more goods on to the black market, and their efforts to improve supply by bulk purchase were frustrated by lack of funds.

The Union of Towns, representing town councils, several times approached the Special Council for Supply seeking an overall plan to overcome the shortages by improving distribution. However, the Council, though specifically charged with 'co-ordinating all measures relating to problems of supplying the army and civilian population, and all institutions concerned with the same', proved reluctant to follow that line, mainly because the information needed for control was not available. Only in February 1916 did it introduce a draft scheme combining price control with regulation of rail transport, providing for rationing if necessary, and taking an agricultural census to provide the information needed for controlling prices and regulating supply.

This attempt to control the crisis was belated and inadequate. In particular, the local machinery for the supply scheme proved unworkable, mainly because it had separate commissioners to control supply to the army and the civilian population, and these acted independently, often competing with one another. Some imposed prices fixed arbitrarily or under pressure from interested parties. Others published permissible profit margins, thereby tempting merchants to inflate costs so as to increase profits. Yet others banned all price increases, and introduced severe penalties for offenders. Since some increases were inevitable, this drove commodities on to the black market.

Nor was it possible to co-ordinate and systematise freight transport, because of the overstrained railways and the priority accorded military traffic. In the Moscow Regional Committee's six provinces, for example, shipments in June 1916 were only 34.9 per cent of those planned. In most areas the 1916 grain harvest was excellent, but supply barely improved because landlords hoarded the grain to secure higher winter prices. Inevitably, bread shortages in towns, alongside known abundance of grain, strained urban–rural relations. The municipalities justly accused landlords and peasants of profiteering, while rural spokesmen pointed out equally justly that controlling prices of food but not of industrial products was discriminatory.

Amidst mutual recriminations, supply continued to deteriorate. The moneyed classes could eat well on food bought on the black market or brought from their estates, but for the ordinary citizen late 1916 was a time of 'queuing for thirteen hours for black bread, and living on cereals and porridge'. This continued until the run-down railways finally buckled under the cold in February 1917, and the food riots in March swiftly escalated into demands for the 'Nemka' ('German woman' – the Tsaritsa) to be removed and the Tsar to abdicate.

By then Petrograd had shed its urbanity. Streets lay uncleared of snow. Improvised stove-pipes poked out of windows because heating systems had broken down for lack of coal and the residents were making do with wood-burning stoves. There were no trams, almost no street lighting, and queues for bread outside bakers' shops formed before dawn.

Under the Provisional Government urban living conditions got even worse. By July 1917 the price of bread had trebled and of potatoes, shoes and clothing more than trebled, while wages had risen by only one-third. Fuel and raw materials shortages, and cancelled orders, saw 568 firms in Petrograd close by July, throwing over 100,000 out of work. The workers' response was to establish factory committees to oversee owners, managers and accountants, and by August these were Bolshevik dominated. The Bolshevik seizure of power and consequent peace treaty brought some easing, but the Civil War soon broke out, and nothing resembling normal conditions returned to Russia's towns for at least another two years.

# The Bolsheviks seize power

The Russian Empire began to break up after the Bolsheviks seized power. The Ukrainian Rada declared independence on 22 January 1918, and on 9 February Germany signed a peace treaty with it, together with an economic deal for delivery of a million tons of grain to Germany and Austria-Hungary. When Soviet government forces drove the Rada from Kiev, the Germans invaded Ukraine because they needed its grain, iron ore and coal to mitigate the effects of the blockade. Ukrainian co-operation was not sought; instead German firms were brought in to run Ukraine's mines and railways, and a puppet regime under the aptly named Skoropadsky ('quick-fall') was installed. The Germans' demands for food supplies alienated the peasants; their arrogance and profiteering alienated the industrial and mine workers. Saboteurs proliferated, so did Bolshevik propaganda, the German commander, Field-Marshal von Eichhorn, was assassinated in July 1918, and when the Germans withdrew following the November Armistice, their puppet regime quickly fell.

Finland declared independence soon after the Bolsheviks seized power. Although this action had Lenin's approval, a civil war

The cruiser *Goeben*, which along with the *Breslau* was employed by the Turks in attacking Russian Black Sea ports on 29 October 1914. (Ann Ronan Picture Library)

broke out in January 1918. The 'Reds' seized Helsinki and a 'White' government was formed in the north, with small forces under Mannerheim, a former Russian army general. He appealed to Germany for help, and a German division arrived in April. With its help the Reds were beaten before the year's end, but Germany's defeat aborted plans to install a German prince as king. Mannerheim became regent, and a republic was proclaimed in July 1919 and formally recognised by Soviet Russia in the 1920 Treaty of Tartu.

The Kaiser wanted to annex the former Russian Baltic provinces (Estonia, Courland, Livonia and Lithuania) to Prussia. The Reichstag wanted to annex them to the Reich. A group within the Foreign Office advocated their independence as non-Communist states which, being small and economically dominated by ethnic German 'Baltic barons', would naturally gravitate towards Germany rather than Russia. Bolshevik sympathies were widespread among the locals, and German behaviour during the occupation tended to alienate them.

The 'barons' set up pseudo-parliaments, lobbied influential relatives in Germany, especially in the army, and appealed to the Kaiser to intervene. In February 1918, German troops went in as 'peacekeepers', and made secret deals with the biggest barons to have

German troops arrest suspected Bolsheviks. (Edimedia, Paris)

the pseudo-parliaments declare independence, then immediately vote for annexation by Germany. These moves were frustrated by Germany's defeat, and after its surrender the provinces became the independent states of Estonia, Latvia and Lithuania.

Harsh as was the Treaty of Brest-Litovsk, German behaviour was even harsher. Lenin had agreed to the treaty because Russia had no choice, with an army whose will to fight had been destroyed largely by his own propaganda; in any case, he believed the other belligerents would soon follow Russia's example, and the treaty would then lapse. He was right on the last point, though wrong about the reason for it.

Germany's behaviour in the east in 1918 did nothing to help it win the war, and may have helped Germany to lose it. The 100-plus German and Austro-Hungarian Eastern Front divisions used to further plans for annexations there would not have been needed if the Russian Empire had simply been left to disintegrate. They could have been shipped to the Western Front and almost doubled the force available for the 1918 spring offensive, the Central Powers' last chance of winning before the Americans arrived.

Paradoxically, it was the military's dominance in German decision-making that brought about this militarily counter-productive situation. Initially Hindenburg and Ludendorff sought a quick conclusion to the Brest-Litovsk negotiations precisely so that they could transfer troops to

Carl Gustaf Mannerheim. (AKG Berlin)

the West as soon as possible. But they kept the troops at hand to pressure the Russian negotiators because they wanted a peace that reflected the completeness of their victory. In seeking it they behaved as if they had already won the whole war, rather than just what they agreed was the less important half of it. The stick used to beat the Bolshevik negotiators was the threat that if Germany's demands were not met, the advance would resume, and the treaty not negotiated at Brest-Litovsk would be dictated in Petrograd.

The German government was less ambitious than the military. Foreign Minister von Kühlmann did not share the generals' belief that complete victory was possible. Even if German arms were victorious on the Western Front, Germany did not have the sea power to confront the world's two strongest navies and invade the United Kingdom, its Dominions or the United States. Peace could be imposed on Russia and France by victory on land, but peace with the 'Anglo-Saxons' would at best have to be negotiated. Von Kühlmann was as keen as the generals to take territory in the east, but only to use as bargaining counters in peace negotiations, by offering to yield territory there in order to avoid having to do so in

A German armoured train in Finland, 1918. (Ann Ronan Picture Library)

the west. He also wanted a settlement with the Russians that would not be held against Germany by its future negotiating partners.

So when the new Soviet government invited all the belligerents to negotiate peace on the basis of 'no annexations, no indemnities, and the principle of self-determination', Kühlmann and his Austrian counterpart, von Czernin, agreed. But when the other Entente powers rejected the formula, leaving Russia to negotiate alone, the German military insisted not only on a speedy settlement, but on a victor's peace that extracted as much as possible from the vanquished.

The Soviet delegation, headed by Trotsky, was motivated to prolong the negotiations as much as possible, to give time for the proletariat and peasantry in the other belligerent countries to absorb and, they hoped, copy the example of Russia's Bolshevik revolution. Trotsky succeeded in dragging negotiations out for six weeks. But on 9 February 1918, the Central Powers forced his hand, by recognising Ukraine as independent, and signing a peace treaty that made it a virtual protectorate and an agreement for it to deliver 1 million tons of food to Germany and Austria-Hungary. On the next day Trotsky declared the war ended but the Central Powers' terms rejected, proclaimed 'neither war nor peace' and left

# The front line at peace and after

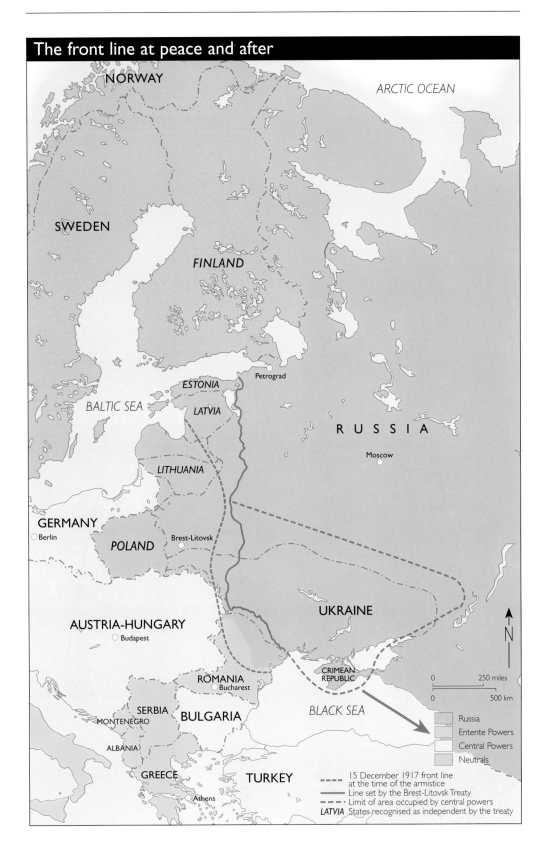

NORWAY

ARCTIC OCEAN

SWEDEN

FINLAND

BALTIC SEA

ESTONIA

Petrograd

LATVIA

RUSSIA

Moscow

LITHUANIA

GERMANY

Berlin

POLAND

Brest-Litovsk

UKRAINE

AUSTRIA-HUNGARY

Budapest

N

CRIMEAN
REPUBLIC

ROMANIA

Bucharest

0        250 miles

0        500 km

SERBIA

MONTENEGRO

BULGARIA

BLACK SEA

Russia

Entente Powers

ALBANIA

Central Powers

Neutrals

GREECE

TURKEY

Athens

- - - - -  15 December 1917 front line
at the time of the armistice
━━━━━  Line set by the Brest-Litovsk Treaty
- - - -  Limit of area occupied by central powers
*LATVIA*  States recognised as independent by the treaty

A WALK-OVER?

THE KAISER. "THIS IS THE DOORMAT OF OUR NEW PREMISES."
EMPEROR KARL. "ARE YOU QUITE SURE IT'S DEAD?"

Cartoon, originally from Punch. (Ann Ronan Picture Library)

for Petrograd, apparently believing that the
Central Powers needed peace as much as
Russia did, and would soon come to heel.

All his flamboyant gesture achieved
was to hand the initiative back from the
diplomats to the soldiers. Despite strong
protests by Kühlmann and Czernin,
Hindenburg and Ludendorff secured the

The signing of the Russo-German peace treaty at Brest-Litovsk, 2 March 1918. (Ann Ronan Picture Library)

Kaiser's reluctant consent to resuming hostilities. What remained of Russia's army melted away before the German troops, who advanced to within 80 miles (130km) of Petrograd in a few days, virtually unopposed. The Bolsheviks then gave in and asked for peace terms. The Germans set them out as an ultimatum to be accepted within three days, and a treaty to be ratified within two weeks of signing. The Bolshevik leadership was split, and Lenin had some trouble in getting his own way. But in reality they had no choice but to comply, and the Treaty of Brest-Litovsk was signed on 3 March 1918.

It was a very punitive treaty. Russia had to recognise the independence of Finland, Ukraine and Georgia, yield sovereignty over its four Baltic provinces and adjacent islands to Germany, over Russian Poland to Germany and Austria-Hungary, over Kars, Ardahan and Batum to Turkey, and pay six billion Marks in reparations. Since Marx had predicted that the socialist revolution was most likely to happen first in highly industrialised countries, Lenin signed in the belief that it would soon be rendered inoperative by revolutions throughout Europe. In fact, it and the supplementary treaty of August became inoperative before the year was out, as a result not of revolution, but of Germany's defeat by the capitalist Entente powers. Both treaties were annulled on 13 November, two days after the Armistice.

But even that Armistice did not bring peace to Russia. The Allied forces which in the first instance had come primarily to prevent the handover of military supplies to the Germans, and to keep the Caspian oilfields out of German hands, did not leave when the war's end removed the threat. The prospect of strangling the Communist state at birth would lead to increasing foreign interventions on the side of the 'Whites' in the ensuing Civil War. To win that war the Bolsheviks, who had subverted the old army during 1917, and dissolved it in 1918, would now have to build the new 'Workers' and Peasants' Red Army' from its remnants.

# The emergence of a superpower

Russia did not collapse because of a bloodbath. Estimates of its war dead range between half a million and two million, but even the higher figure equals only one dead per 83 of population, and the more generally accepted figure of 1.45 million equals only 1 per 115. This is by far the lowest ratio among the major belligerents, compared with the French of 1 per 28 of population, German 1 in 32, Austro-Hungarian 1 in 56, and British 1 in 57.

A measure of the relative effectiveness of the Entente's armies can be deduced by comparing German casualty figures for the two major fronts. Over the war period Germany committed fewer than twice as many divisions to the Western Front as it did to the Eastern; but its 1,214,100 dead or missing in the west were 3.8 times the 317,100 dead or missing in the east. A German soldier on the Eastern Front was therefore nearly twice as likely to survive as one on the Western. He was also over five times as likely to survive as a Russian, and that is more significant. A Russian front-line soldier could time after time see for himself how the Germans could kill, wound or capture Russians at little cost to himself because he had more artillery, more machine guns and ample supplies of ammunition for both, as well as for his personal weapon.

Austria-Hungary lost 905,299 dead, 60 per cent of them on the Eastern Front, and 837,483 missing. The latter figure was revised to 181,000 after the war, since most of the missing turned out to be Slav troops who had surrendered or defected. During 1917–18 many Russian units dissolved spontaneously because peasant soldiers went home to ensure they did not miss out on land redistribution resulting from break-up of the landlords' estates. Others left because they saw no point in staying, illustrating the difficulty in a very large country of obtaining national unity. In the 1904–05 war with Japan, Russian observers complained that only soldiers from east of Lake Baikal took the war seriously; conversely, in 1917–18 the Siberian regiments were the first to leave the front, on the grounds that 'the Germans won't be coming to Siberia'.

Like the figures for deaths, those for Russian prisoners of war and missing vary considerably. The most authoritative post-war study gave 3,409,433 captured and 228,838 missing. When the figures for captured or missing are placed alongside the figures of dead, the Russian army differs markedly from the other major belligerents. For every 100 dead in 1914–18 Russia had 251 captured or missing, Austria-Hungary 150, Italy 92, Germany 65, France 46 and British/British Empire forces 21. In other words, Russian soldiers far more often than others were either led into situations where capture was inevitable, or were very much readier to surrender than others.

The course of events and the military censorship reports tend to indicate that failures of generalship accounted for most captures in 1914–15, and readiness to surrender for most in 1916–17. Put briefly, the early débâcles eroded the soldiers' faith in their leaders and willingness to fight for the regime that they represented. The British Military Attaché, Major-General Knox, once remarked that Russian army training placed too much emphasis on dying for the country, and not enough on conquering for it. It appears to have failed in both respects; even at the lowest point in French morale, the mutineers of 1917, though refusing to attack, neither refused to defend nor abandoned the front en masse. Russians did both.

A number of factors additional to war-weariness contributed to the rapid decline of Russia's armies during 1917. Two bodies, the Provisional Government and the Petrograd Soviet, contended for their allegiance; the Germans skilfully fomented revolution by facilitating Lenin's return from Switzerland, and, at the front, allowed fraternisation, dissemination of propaganda and abstention from active operations to reduce the Russian soldier's will to fight. The Provisional Government's efforts to continue an unpopular war without being able to restore officers' disciplinary powers also contributed. So did Bolshevik and Left SR fostering of the delusion that peace 'without annexations or indemnities' was possible, so that Russia could hope for a painless exit from the war. But in the final analysis, these only accelerated the inevitable, since it was already evident by October 1916 that Russia's manpower was almost exhausted. By then, available reserves, at 1.4 million, were less than enough for another five months of war, so that after February 1917 the Russian army would be living on borrowed time.

It was the manpower losses of 1914–16 that caused the decline of 1917. They in turn were caused by Tsarist Russia's inability to conduct a modern war, in which good generalship had to be supported by immense quantities of artillery and ammunition, and backed by a sophisticated logistical system, which could not only feed and supply the armies in the field, but maintain the civilian population at reasonable standards of diet and morale. Too often the Russian infantryman was called on to retake with blood what the German had taken with high explosive, and by the spring of 1917 he had had enough.

The seeds of the revolution had been sown at Tannenberg, the Mazurian Lakes, Gorlice-Tarnów and a score of lesser disasters. In 1916 morale was finding it hard to accept even the casualties that went with victory, and when the Romanian débâcle nullified the Brusilov offensive's gains, it, too, was remembered for its casualties rather than its achievements. But the manpower losses were not caused by exceptional sacrifices. All the major belligerents except the late-arriving United States had a higher proportion of their populations killed than did Russia. But they also had far fewer surrenders.

Along with the drain on manpower went growing hardship among the civilian population. The country possessed abundant food and fuel, but had a railway network unable to cope with the increased wartime traffic, and so badly managed that its capacity to move freight actually declined by more than half in less than three years. Ultimately, the armed forces' losses and the civilians' hardships combined to produce massive disenchantment with the war and the regime that had taken them into it.

The hastily assembled Provisional Government had to contend from the outset with an alternative source of power, the Petrograd Soviet, which the Bolsheviks ultimately came to dominate, and try in addition to reconcile the irreconcilable. On the one hand, the country wanted out of the war, and was encouraged by Bolshevik and Left SR propaganda to think it could get out painlessly. On the other, the British, French and Italians were desperate to keep the Eastern Front alive, for fear of what additional enemy divisions could do if they arrived in the West before the Americans. They also failed to appreciate that there was no substantial body within Russia that wanted to fight on. They showered Russia with money and military supplies in quantities that if applied earlier, while the railways could still move them, might have prevented the collapse.

The Provisional Government, well aware that a Central Powers victory would see autocracy restored, tried to meet its Allies' wishes, and thereby brought on a disaster more complete even than those that had resulted from Russia's responses to French and Italian appeals for help. The July offensive was a fiasco, and with few exceptions, the troops thereafter refused to fight.

Romania's fate was a mere footnote to Russia's, but the Treaty of Bucharest (7 May 1918) was even more draconian than that of Brest-Litovsk. Its Carpathian provinces were ceded to Hungary, its coastline and control of the Danube to Germany and Austria-Hungary, southern Dobrudja to an Austro-German condominium, northern Dobrudja to Bulgaria. Romania was to supply the Central Powers with foodstuffs at fixed (low) prices for several years, and give Germany a 99-year lease on its oil wells. Fortunately for Romania, this treaty too was invalidated by the Central Powers' defeat.

The treaties imposed on Russia and Romania give some indication of what the British and French could have expected if they had lost the war. They also put into perspective the alleged harshness of the Treaty of Versailles which the Nazis, among others, would exploit in the inter-war period to harness German nationalism for another war of aggression.

The consequences of the First World War in the east included the restoration of an independent Poland, the severance of East Prussia from the rest of Germany by the Polish Corridor, independence of the three Baltic States and Finland, and dismembering of the Russian, Habsburg and Ottoman Empires. The settlement would in due course prove to have created more problems than it solved, because the new states mostly contained ethnic minorities and/or territories that could be subjects of irredentist claims by Germany or the Soviet Union.

Ukraine, Georgia, Eastern Poland, Estonia, Latvia, Lithuania, some Finnish territory, Bessarabia and part of Bukovina (from Romania), and Ruthenia (from Czechoslovakia) all came under Soviet rule under Stalin, whose revolutionary rhetoric covered an ambition to restore and even extend the frontiers of the former Russian Empire as much as possible. In post-Second World War negotiations he revived, though he did not pursue, Nicholas' claim for control of the Turkish Straits, and sought the return of Kars and Ardahan.

Hitler's ambitions in the east went far beyond the Kaiser's, and included annexation of all former Russian Empire territory west of the Ural Mountains. The belief that this could be achieved by military means was based mainly on Stalin's purge of the Red Army's leadership in 1937–38, and that army's poor performance in the war with Finland in 1939–40. But it was underpinned by the belief that these events showed the Red Army to be no better than its Tsarist predecessor, and therefore as beatable as that predecessor.

Probably the major consequence was the creation of the Soviet Union. A bitter civil war resulted in the replacement of a self-proclaimed autocracy by an autocracy, then an oligarchy, that both claimed to be democratic and socialist, and of a self-proclaimed empire by an empire that claimed to be the arch-enemy of empires. Stalin's autocracy would prove far more oppressive than that of Nicholas II, but also much more efficient at harnessing the nation's resources and industrialising its economy. In 1941–45 the Soviet Union would experience losses of people and territory far greater than those that brought down Tsarism. But it would emerge a victorious superpower, form a bloc of satellite states, and remain a superpower until in 1991 the empire collapsed yet again, leaving post-Soviet Russia with western frontiers closely resembling those imposed by the Treaty of Brest-Litovsk.

# Further reading

Brusilov, A., *A Soldier's Notebook*, London, MacMillan, 1930.

Cowles, V., *The Kaiser*, New York, Harper & Row, 1963.

Golovine, N., *The Russian Army in the World War*, Oxford, Oxford University Press, 1931.

*History of the First World War* (8 vols), London, Purnell, 1969-71.

Knox, A., *With the Russian Army 1914–1917*, New York, Dutton, 1921.

Ludendorff, E., *My War Memories 1914–1918*, London, Hutchinson, 1919.

Massie, R. K., *Nicholas and Alexandra*, London, Gollancz, 1968.

# Index

References to illustrations are shown in **bold**.

Alexandra, Tsaritsa **11**, 12, 38, 77, 79
Alexandrovsk (Murmansk) 76, 79
Alexey **11**, 12
Alexeyev, General Mikhail **26**, 26, 38, 42, 44, 45, 48, 50,
    51, 61, 62
Allied interventions 79
Anatolia 39
Anglo-Russian Convention 11
Archangel 76, 79
Armistice 68, 89
Austria-Hungary 24, 38, 81 *see also* Central Powers
Austrian Army
    First Army 25, 26
    Second Army 24, 28, 42, 45
    Third Army 24, 26, 29, 34, 35-36
    Fourth Army 29, 34, 45
    Seventh Army 48, 51
Austro-Hungarian Dual Monarchy 15, 29
Austro-Hungarian forces 45, 69
    soldiers and equipment 16

Baltic provinces 84-85, 92
Bergmann, General 29
Bezobrazov, General 49
Black Sea 41-42
Bolsheviks 67, 68, 74, 79-80, 83, **85**
    seize power 84-89
Bothmer 50
Brudermann, General 24
Brusilov, General Alexey **23**, 29, 33, 34, 35, 63, 64, 77
Brusilov offensive 42-50, **43**, 77
Buchanan, ambassador 55
Bulgaria 15, 38, 50 *see also* Central Powers

Carpathians, Eastern 33-34, **34**
casualties *see* losses
Central Powers 48, 49, 50, 52, 79, 85, 86, 91
    advance 64-68
Civil War, Russian 89
Conrad von Hötzendorff, Field-Marshal **12**, 15, 16, 23, 24,
    25-26, 28, 29, 34
Czechs 69, **70-71**
Czernowitz (Chernivtsi) 48

Dniestr river 45, 49
Dobrudja 50, 51, 52
Draft Military Convention 8
Dvina river, German crossing of **64-65**, 66

Eastern Front 34, 42, 61, 62, 91
Ekonomiya 76
ensign, Russian, experiences of 69-70, 75
Enver Pasha **15**, 15, 18, 29
Erzerum 41
Evert, General 44, 45, 48

Falkenhayn, General von **24**, 24-25, 28, 30, 34, 35, 38, 42,
    52, 77
Ferdinand, Archduke Franz 15, 16
Finland 13, 84
First World War, consequences of 92
food prices 82
food riots in Petrograd **56-57**, 56
Franco-Russian Conventions 8
Franz Josef, Emperor 26
front line at peace and after **87**

Galicia, Russian offensive in 22-25, **31**, 36
Gallipoli 38, 76
German Army
    Third Army 28, 33
    Eighth Army 19, 20, 22, 25, 30, 31-32, 33, 34, 65
    Ninth Army 25, 26, 28, 52
    Tenth Army 30, 32

Eleventh Army 34, 35
'Army Group Mackensen' 35
    crossing of the Dvina river **64-65**, 66
    High Command 16
    soldiers and equipment 16, 17, **54**, 69, **80**, **85**
    Southern Army 33, 45
Germany *see also* Central Powers
    conditions 81
    expansion 15
    strategy 24
*Goeben*, cruiser **84**
Gorbatov, Trooper Alexander 75 *see also* trooper, Russian,
    experiences of
Gorlice-Tarnów, breakthrough at 34-36, **35**
Greece 73
Guchkov, War Minister 61, 62
Gurko, General 42, 54

Hasan Izzet Pasha 29, 30
Hindenburg, General 19, **20**, 25, 28, 30, 33, 49, 52, 85-86,
    88-89
Hitler, Adolf 92
Hoffman, Colonel (later General) 20, **22**, 22, 68
horses 18
hospital, military **72**
Hötzendorff, Field-Marshal von *see* Conrad von
    Hötzendorff, Field-Marshal
Hutier, General von 66

infantry
    German 69
    Romanian **51**
    Russian **46-47**, 69
Iran 8
Ivanov 26, 29, 31, 33, 44

Japan 7, 11
Jaroslaw, Battle of 35

Kaledin, General 45, 48, 68
Kerensky, War Minister (later Prime Minister) 61, **62**, 63,
    64, 67-68
Khabalov, General 57, 58
Klembovsky, General 66
Komaróv, Battle of 24
Köprüköy 41
Kornilov, General 64, **66**, 68
Kovel 48-49
Krivoshein 38
Kronstadt, Battle of **52-53**, 52
Krylenko **68**, 68
Kühlmann, Foreign Minister von 86
Kuropatkin, General 44
Kutno, Battle of 28

Lechitsky 45, 48, 50, 52-53
Lemberg, Battle of 36
Lenin (Vladimir Ilyich Ulyanov) 60, **61**, **63**, 74, **78**, 79, 85,
    89, 91
Limanowa-Lapanów, Battle of 29, **30**
Lódz, Battle of 26-29, **27**
losses 22, 24, 30, 38, 50, 90
    Russian 33, 36, 41, 42, 54, 73
Ludendorff, General 19, **20**, 25-26, 44, 85-86, 88-89

Mackensen, Field-Marshal von **25**, 25, 26, 34, 36, 52
Mannerheim, General Carl Gustav 84, **85**
Masurian Lakes, Battle of the 22, **23**
Mesopotamia (Iraq) 39
mobilisation 8, 12, 73
Moltke 19, 24
Mus 41

Naval Conventions 8
Nicholas II, Tsar **11**, 11, 12, 37-38, 44, 53, 55, 59-60, 69, 77
Nikolay, Grand Duke **19**, 19, 25, 26, 29, 31, 35, 36, 74

appointed Viceroy and Commander in the Caucasus 38, 39
'scorched earth' policy **36-37**, 37, 38

Petrograd 12, 83
   food riots **56-57**, 56
   Garrison 60, 73, 74, 75
   Military Censorship Commission 73
   Soviet (Council) **59**, 59, 60, 62, 91 *see also* 'Soviet of
   Workers' and Soldiers' Deputies'
Pflanzer-Baltin, General 33-34, 35, 48
Poland 13, 15
Polish village, burning **36-37**
Polivanov, General 37, 77
priest **72**
prisoners-of-war *see* losses
Prittwitz, General von 19
'Progressive Bloc' 77
Protopopov, Alexander 79
Provisional Government 59, 60, 62-63, 67, 79, 91
Prussia 16
Prussia, East 31-33
   Russian invasion of 19-22, 25
Prut river 48
Przemysl **32-33**, 33, 34

radio, Russia's use of 20, 25
railways, German 16 *see also* 'Sealed Train'; train, German
   armoured
railways, Russian 76-77, 79, 91 *see also* Trans-Siberian
   Railway
Rasputin, Grigoriy **12**, 12, 38, 77, 79
Rava Russkaya-Zolkiew line 36
refugees 36-37
Rennenkampf, General 19, 20, 22, 28
Rodzyanko 55, 60
Romania 15, 50, 52, 54, 77, 81
Romanian campaign 50-54, **55**, 91-92
Romanian Front 54, 64
Romanian infantry **51**, **52-53**
Rushsky 29, 31
Russia 11-13, **14**
   alignment with British and French Empires 7-8
   Black Sea Fleet 42
   coal supplies 76
   conditions 81-83
   expansion 7
   food shortages 82-83
   religion 13
   Siberian Air Squadron 39
   Tsarist, last days of 76-80
Russian Army
   First Army 19, 20, 22, 25, 26, 28, 42
   Second Army 19-20, 22, 25, 26, 28
   Third Army 23, 26, 28, 29, 34, 35, 48, 49
   Fourth Army 23, 25, 26, 44
   Fifth Army 24, 25, 26, 42
   Seventh Army 45, 49, 50, 51-52, 55
   Eighth Army 23, 26, 29, 44, 45, 48, 49, 54, 55, 64
   Ninth Army 23-24, 25, 26, 29, 35, 45, 48, 49, 50, 52,
   53-54, 55
   Tenth Army 22, 25, 26, 31, 44
   Eleventh Army 26, 33, 45, 48, 49, 51, 64
   Twelfth Army 31, 42, 65
   Army of the Caucasus 29
   Caucasian Rifle Division, 4th 41
   cavalry **40-41**, 68
   Cossacks 56, 68
   Danube Army 54
   desertions 45, 82
   'Dobrudja Detachment' 51, 54
   equipment 17-18
   Guard Army 44, 49
   infantry **46-47**, 69 *see also* Russian Army, soldiers
   Pavlovsky Life Guard Regiment 57
   Red Army 92
   retreat 36-38
   soldiers 17, **20-21**, **46-47**, 69, 71-72, **75**
      mutiny 73, 75
   Special Army 49, 51, 54, 73
   Stavka (GHQ) 23, 24, 25, 28, 42, 48, 74

supplies 76
   volunteer shock battalions 64
   women's battalion **18**
Russian Empire, break up of 84
Russian Fronts
   home front, 1917: 55-63
   North Front 42, 44, 54, 64
   North-West Front 29
   Romanian Front 54, 64
   South-West Front 29, 36, 44, 45, 48, 51, 53, 54, 64, 69
   West Front 28, 34, 42, 44, 54, 61, 62, 64
Russian offensive in Turkey 38-42
Russian parliament (Duma) 59, **60**, 77
Russo-Japanese War 7, 11

Sakharov, General 54
Samsonov, General 19, 20, 22
Sanok, Battle of 35
Sarikamis, Battle of 30
Sazonov, Foreign Minister 77
Scheffer, General 28
'Sealed Train' 60, **62**
Serbia 38
sergeant, Russian, experiences of 69, 70-71, 72-73, 75
Shuvayev, General 44, 77
Souchon, Admiral 15, 18
'Soviet of Workers' and Soldiers' Deputies' 60, 62, 68 *see
   also* Petrograd Soviet
Soviet poster **78**
Soviet Union, creation of 92
Stalin, Josef **63**, 92
Steppe, Governates of 7
Stokhod river 49
Stürmer, Prime Minister 77
superpower, emergence of 90-92
Supply, Special Council for 82-83

Tannenberg, Battle of **20-21**, 22, **23**
Trabzon, fall of **39**, **40-41**, 42
train, German armoured **86**
Trans-Siberian Railway **14**, **70-71**, 76
Transylvania 50, 52
treaties
   Brest-Litovsk 79, 80, 85, 86, **89**, 89
   Bucharest 91-92
   London 79
   Tartu 84
   Triple Alliance 7
   Versailles 92
trooper, Russian, experiences of 69, 70, 74-75
Trotsky 86, 88
Turkey 15, 79
   British and French support in the Crimea 7
   Russian offensive in, winter 1915-16: 38-42
Turkish Army 15, 18
   Second Army 42
   Third Army 15, 29, 38-39, 41, 42
Turkish front, winter 1914-15: 29-30
Turkish Straits 7, 11, 15, 29, 76

Ukraine **80**, 81, 82, 84, 86

Vasilevsky, Ensign Alexander 75 *see also* ensign, Russian,
   experiences of
Vilnius 42, 44
Vistula line 19, 25, 36
Vladimir-Volynski 54
Vladivostok 76, 79

Warsaw, Battles of 25-26, 36 *see also* Lódz, Battle of
'Warsaw bulge' 16, 22, 23
Wilhelm II, Kaiser 11, 24, 26, **67**, 84, **88**, 88-89
winter campaigns, 1915: 30-34, **34**
Winter Palace, storming of **58**, 58

Yudenich, General 38, 39, 41

Zhiglinsky, Alexander 72, 75
Zhukov, Sergeant Georgiy 75 *see also* sergeant, Russian,
   experiences of

# Other titles in the Essential Histories series

**The Crusades**
ISBN 1 84176 179 6

**The Crimean War**
ISBN 1 84176 186 9

**The Seven Years'
War**
ISBN 1 84176 191 5

**The Napoleonic
Wars** The rise of the
Emperor 1805–1807
ISBN 1 84176 205 9

**The Napoleonic
Wars** The empires fight
back 1808–1812
ISBN 1 84176 298 9

**The French
Revolutionary Wars**
ISBN 1 84176 283 0

**Campaigns of the
Norman Conquest**
ISBN 1 84176 228 8

**The American Civil
War** The war in the
East 1861–May 1863
ISBN 1 84176 239 3

**The American Civil
War** The war in the
West 1861–July 1863
ISBN 1 84176 240 7

**The American Civil
War** The war in the
East 1863–1865
ISBN 1 84176 241 5

**The American Civil
War** The war in the
West 1863–1865
ISBN 1 84176 242 3

**The Korean War**
ISBN 1 84176 282 2

**The First World War**
The Eastern Front
1914–1918
ISBN 1 84176 342 X
**January 2002**

**The First World War**
The Western Front
1914–1916
ISBN 1 84176 347 0
**January 2002**

**The Punic Wars
264–146 BC**
ISBN 1 84176 355 1
**February 2002**

**The Falklands
War 1982**
ISBN 1 84176 422 1
**February 2002**

**The Napoleonic
Wars** The Peninsular
War 1807–1814
ISBN 1 84176 370 5
**March 2002**

**The Second World
War** The Pacific
ISBN 1 84176 229 6
**March 2002**

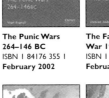

**The Iran-Iraq War
1980–1988**
ISBN 1 84176 371 3
**April 2002**

**The Hundred Years'
War**
ISBN 1 84176 269 5
**June 2002**

**The First World War**
The Western Front
1916–1918
ISBN 1 84176 348 9
**June 2002**

**Rome at War**
AD 229–696
ISBN 1 84176 359 4
**June 2002**

**The First World War**
The Mediterranean
Front 1914–1923
ISBN 1 84176 373 X
**July 2002**

**The Second World
War** The Eastern Front
1941–1945
ISBN 1 84176 391 8
**July 2002**

**The Mexican War
1846–1848**
ISBN 1 84176 472 8
**July 2002**

## Praise for Essential Histories

'clear and concise' *History Today*

'an excellent series' *Military Illustrated*

'Osprey must be congratulated on Essential Histories' *Soldier*

'very useful, factual and educational' *Reference Reviews*

'valuable as an introduction for students or younger readers …
older readers will also find something 'essential' to their understanding' *Star Banner*

'accessible and well illustrated…' *Daily Express*

'… clearly written …' *Oxford Times*

'they make the perfect starting point for readers of any age' *Daily Mail*

**The Wars of
Alexander the Great**
ISBN 1 84176 473 6
**July 2002**

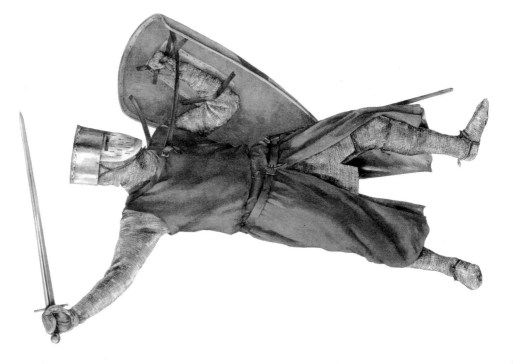

# FIND OUT MORE ABOUT OSPREY

❏ Please send me a FREE trial issue of Osprey Military Journal

❏ Please send me the latest listing of Osprey's publications

❏ I would like to subscribe to Osprey's e-mail newsletter

Title/rank

Name

Address

Postcode/zip

State/country

E-mail

Which book did this card come from?

❏ I am interested in military history

My preferred period of military history is

❏ I am interested in military aviation

My preferred period of military aviation is

I am interested in (please tick all that apply)

❏ general history     ❏ militaria     ❏ model making

❏ wargaming     ❏ re-enactment

Please send to:

**USA & Canada**:
Osprey Direct USA, c/o Motorbooks International,
PO Box 1, 729 Prospect Avenue, Osceola, WI 54020, USA

**UK, Europe and rest of world**:
Osprey Direct UK, PO Box 140, Wellingborough,
Northants, NN8 2FA, United Kingdom

www.ospreypublishing.com

call our telephone hotline
for a free information pack

USA & Canada: 1-800-458-0454
UK, Europe and rest of world call:
+44 (0) 1933 443 863

**Young Guardsman**
Figure taken from *Warrior 22:*
*Imperial Guardsman 1799–1815*
Published by Osprey
Illustrated by Richard Hook

Rec'd 7/30/02 # 14.95

POSTCARD

**Knight, c.1190**
Figure taken from *Warrior 1: Norman Knight 950 – 1204AD*
Published by Osprey
Illustrated by Christa Hook